Praise for

The Reincarnation Controversy

The subject of reincarnation is one of the most misunderstood in the popular imagination. Steven Rosen's book, *The Reincarnation Controversy: Uncovering the Truth in the World Religions*, clears up many myths and stereotypes and presents in a concise form the many types of reincarnationist thought found in the major world religions. It is a pleasure to see so many sources collected and summarized into a nice small volume, which will be effective in educating students and public readers alike.

> —Dr. Guy L. Beck, Dept. of
> Religious Studies,
> Loyola University

Reincarnation, or the transmigration of the soul, is a path every person travels. This book is a thorough discourse on the science of reincarnation, and a most valuable book for any person who desires to know who they are, why things happen to them and what they can do to ensure a better life in the present and the future.

> —Terry Cole-Whittaker, D.D.,
> *New York Times* listed best-selling
> author, *How to Have More
> in a Have Not World*

This eminently readable book surveys the evidence for the existence of the soul and its migration through lives as expounded by all the major religious traditions. Anyone who reads this book will understand more clearly the nature and purpose of their own journey through life and death.

> —Pandit Rajmani Tigunait, Ph.D.
> is the Spiritual Director of the
> Himalayan Institute

First Printing 1997

Cover and book design by Stewart Cannon / Logo Loco Graphics
Printed in the United States of America

Published simultaneously in The United States of America and Canada by Torchlight Publishing

Library of Congress Cataloging-in-Publishing Data
Rosen, Steven, 1955—
    The reincarnation controversy : uncovering the truth in the
    world religions / by Steven Rosen
       p.   cm.
    Includes bibliographical references and index
    ISBN 1-887089-11-X
    1.Reincarnation— Comparative studies.   I. Title.
    BL515.R66   1997   97-18655
    291.2'37– –dc21   CIP

Attention Colleges, Universities, Corporations, Associations and Professional Organizations: *The Reincarnation Controversy* is available at special discounts for bulk purchases for promotions, premiums, fund-raising or educational use. Special books, booklets, or excerpts can be created to suit your specific needs.

For more information contact the Publisher

TorchliqhT PublishiNq, INc.
shifting the paradigm

PO Box 52 Badger CA 93603
Email: Torchlight@compuserve.com
1-888-TorchLt toll free

THE
REINCARNATION
CONTROVERSY

**Uncovering the Truth
in the World Religions**

THE
REINCARNATION
CONTROVERSY

**Uncovering the Truth
in the World Religions**

Steven
Rosen

 Torchlight Publishing, Inc.

shifting the paradigm

Foreword

When people begin to explore the concept of reincarnation as a possible answer to life's fundamental mysteries, they often turn to the teachings of their religions for guidance. In many cases, they may encounter explicit rejection of the concept of a self that can survive the death experience and be reborn in a new physical form. But if they had a chance to look into the history of their own religions, they might be surprised to see that there is no barrier at all to the acceptance of reincarnation. In his insightful and well-researched book, *The Reincarnation Controversy*, Steven Rosen, editor of an important journal of religious studies, gives readers just this chance. He guides them through the history of the world's religions, showing how the teachings of all of them are consistent with the idea of reincarnation. In some cases, the teachings of reincarnation are part of little known esoteric traditions. In other cases, early teachings of reincarnation were covered over by misunderstandings and rival schools of thought. Rosen also reviews the history of reincarnation in Western philosophy, and shows how ancient Greek thinkers may have derived their teachings on reincarnation from contacts with ancient India. Finally, Rosen includes a useful chapter showing scientific evidence for reincarnation, drawing especially on psychiatrist Ian Stevenson's convincing studies of past life memories reported by children. Rosen's scholarly yet readable style makes *The Reincarnation Controversy* an excellent resource for the general public as well as students of religion. Anyone interested in religious views on reincarnation will find this provocative book of immense value. It is just the kind of book one will want to share with friends and relatives.

Michael A. Cremo,
Coauthor of *Coming Back:*
The Science of Reincarnation
May 2, 1997, Los Angeles

Table of contents

Dedication

To my Vrinda,
Whom I have known before,
And whom I will know again.

Acknowledgements

I would like to thank Joshua Greene (Yogeshwar), my editor; Greg Stein and Alister Taylor; Babhru Prabhu; Devadatta and Torchlight; and all of the wonderful mystics and theologians who have elucidated the doctrine of reincarnation prior to me—in many ways this book is merely a new incarnation of information that has appeared before.

Introduction

"What can we know of death,
We who cannot understand life?"
—Gates of Prayer[1]

What is life? When a child is born, we can *see* life, hear the sound of it, feel its warmth. Sometimes the newborn is awake; sometimes not. The child will grow, then die. Where did its life force go? What did her short stay here mean? All living beings are born, and then die. Most of us never know more than that. Because so many answers to the questions of life are shrouded in religious and philosophical mystery, few people take time to consider them deeply. We are born in ignorance, raised by parents who, with rare exception, are themselves confused about the nature of life, and most people leave this life the same way: in ignorance. Is there no choice? Through the centuries, a surprising number of intelligent, non-fanatical thinkers have believed there is.

"I am confident," said Socrates, "that there truly is such a thing as living again, that the living spring from the dead, and that the souls of the dead are in existence." Ralph Waldo Emerson agreed. "The soul,"

1

he wrote, "comes from without into the human body, as into a temporary abode, and it goes out of it anew…it passes into other habitations, for the soul is immortal." Moving on to the the 20th century, *The San Francisco Examiner* of August 26, 1928 quoted: "I adopted the theory of reincarnation when I was twenty-six." This surprising announcement by Henry Ford put him in the ranks of a select group of 18th-, 19th-, and 20th-century Americans—Thomas Edison, Benjamin Franklin, Tom Paine, Henry David Thoreau, and Walt Whitman, among others—who believed that the soul, the energy that animates the body, goes on to a new body when the present body dies.

As we approach the next millennium, acceptance of reincarnation grows ever more widespread. In 1969, a Gallup Poll found that nearly 20 percent of the American public believed in life after death. A similar survey in 1981 revealed that 23 percent of all Americans believed in reincarnation—almost one quarter of the population.[2] The percentage has continued to rise each year. In 1989, research analyst Walter Martin wrote that "the latest survey on reincarnation indicates more than 58 percent of Americans polled either believed in it or believed it to be a distinct possibility."[3] According to a recent survey published in *World Statistics* (July, 1996), "More Americans believe in reincarnation than ever before, and more and more Europeans are accepting the doctrine with increasing frequency." Similar statistics exist in other Western countries. (In the East, four out of five people surveyed embrace the doctrine with full conviction.[4] In total, this accounts for well over half the world's population.)

The reasons for belief in reincarnation are as diverse as the people who defend them. This vast array of believers can be divided into three large categories. The first group consists of part-time enthusiasts who are usually given to but a cursory exploration of the subject; these may be either sincere or insincere seekers, neither knowing little more about reincarnation than can be found in the popular reports of supermarket tabloids. The second group is made up of those who dig a little deeper, who have some intuitive sense of the subject, and perhaps even some experiential knowledge, but they, too, have little substance to support their beliefs. Finally, there are those who seriously pursue the subject and who coherently defend their beliefs, including religionists who know the scriptural basis of reincarnation, and scientists, such as Ian Stevenson, who have thoroughly documented case histories suggestive of transmigration. This book will attempt to rectify the poor image of reincarnation projected by faddists, lend substance to the convictions of well-meaning believers, and balance empiric evidence for reincarnation with the wisdom of scriptural tradition.

Research analysts list three main reasons for the continuing rise in a belief in reincarnation: a growing fascination with and respect for Eastern thought, which has proven the timeliness of its ancient wisdom in other areas, such as holistic medicine; a growing preoccupation in Western cultures with the subject of death; and an appreciation for the validity of past-life therapy.[5] Many also find in reincarnation a natural corollary to their growing disenchantment with materialistic science; they also find mounting evidence of a non-material essence to life, and this fits in neatly with a reincarnationist world view. This book will explore these and other motivations. Our primary focus, however, will be reincarnation as a reality perceived (to greater or lesser degree) by every human being, a reality embraced by the earliest cultural traditions. We shall describe how the concept of reincarnation was originally taught in major religions and how adherents defended it with logic, philosophy, and scriptural wisdom. This last subject forms the body of this work.

The Logic of Reincarnation

Believers in reincarnation share a feeling of rightness, of justice and of logic about coming back. Without it, ours would seem a cruel, random, illogical universe in which one child is born wealthy and another poor, one healthy and another with a terminal disease. Whether or not one believes in God, reincarnation allows us to view the human condition from a broader perspective.

Reincarnation in its various historical traditions consistently suggests that this life is a single frame in a filmstrip of lifetimes, and that the body we have now is not the first but only the most current. Proponents of reincarnation say that the "type and make" of our bodily vehicle are the results of activities performed over the roadway of previous lives, and that the activities performed in this life contribute to the kind of vehicle we will inhabit in our next birth. This principle of current action influencing future lives is called in Sanskrit *karma,* and it is this principle that frames the logic of reincarnation: for every action, the law of *karma* says, there is a reaction, much like Newton's Third Law of Motion. Reincarnation can be seen as the harvesting of the fruits of action: act good, get a good body; act bad, get a bad body. Like buying a new car, acquiring a new "type and make" of body is based in large measure on purchasing ability. Material nature, responding to our desires and actions in this life, prepares our next body. If we have good credit, we can upgrade to a better model, with all the fancier features. Our bodily vehicle will reflect our karmic bank balance. The biblical equivalent would be, "As ye sow, so shall ye reap." In *The Republic* (617e), Plato paraphrased the same principle: "God is blameless: man has chosen his own fate, and this by his actions."

On first appraisal, there seems something cold and mechanical about such logic. It seems too impersonal, too cut-and-dried to be a valid explanation of how things work. Could *karma* be a sort of mechanistic determinism foisted upon helpless human beings? Certainly not. "Karma does not constitute determinism," *The Encyclopedia of Eastern Philosophy and Religion* assures us. "The deeds do indeed determine the manner of rebirth, but not the *actions* of the reborn individual—*karma* provides the situation, not the response to the situation." So the living being still has free will. Deeper study in the world's various religious traditions, however, reveals its beauty and symmetry. Given this context, reincarnation does not occur as an isolated event. It connects seamlessly with *karma* and other universal laws to form a reassuring vision of the universe as a university of life that offers learning and eventual graduation—a far cry from the popular but depressing view of the universe as a chaotic wasteland. The latter vision leaves people powerless; the former empowers us as architects of our own future.

Why is one soul trapped in the body of an animal while another enjoys the advantages of human life? The logic of reincarnation dictates that if we behave like animals in this life, we can have an animal body next time around. One may ask, "Who would want to be an animal?" But our activities belie our true desires, and certain activities—uncurbed appetites of various sorts—are better performed in the more robust animal species. Each body is equipped with a particular sensual forte. The human body falls short of the gazelle's in speed, the pigeon's in sexual prowess, the tiger's in digestive power. Reincarnation suggests that we get what we truly want, what we show we want by our actions. And sometimes a human body will simply not afford us the set of senses we need to fulfill our desires.

We might doubt if a "human soul" could ever inhabit an animal body. Do animals really even have a soul? Anyone who has looked into the eyes of a pet dog or cat knows the answer to this question. A sensitive person can look into the eyes of any living creature and see the primal bonding that exists among all living beings. Whatever animates a human is clearly present in the bodies of all breathing creatures. This was eloquently stated by biologist Edward Sykes:

> All living things go through six phases of life: birth, cultivation, growth, production of by-products (in terms of offspring and/or bodily secretions), dwindling, and, finally, death. Animals and humans go through these phases and so both are "alive," or "possess a soul," at least in a practical sense. To function in life, humans and animals both need physical bodies with five senses in order to taste, touch, see, smell, and hear. In addition, we have emotions, will, and intellect, and these, it may be said, come not from the body but from something more subtle, be it mind or soul....We know that animals exhibit emotions, intelligence, and distinct personalities of their own, too. By this criteria, both people and animals have body and soul. The point is this: there is no reason, in terms of observable evidence, or in terms of logic, for one who believes a human has a soul to deny that an animal has one as well. A person may deny that an animal has a soul, but then he will be hard-pressed to prove that a human has one....It may be argued that animals cannot pursue divinity, but this is quite distinct from saying that they do not have a soul....It is for this reason that most mystical traditions accept the doctrine of transmigration, proclaiming that the life-force of humans may one day appear in lower species and vice versa...[6]

As we shall see, world religions have historically embraced reincarnation, for it describes that ethical, moral behavior leads to rebirth in human form—the only species normally endowed with the intellect suitable for seeking God. Moreover, reincarnation speaks directly to the logic of God's compassion, as it provides repeated opportunity for conditioned (embodied) souls to correct themselves. The scriptural references cited in this book point to a vision shared by adherents of the world's great religions: God is seen as Facilitator, a benign and beneficent Supreme Being who sends helpful hints through saints and scriptures. With their guidance, the seeker of enlightenment can escape from the cycle of rebirth altogether. (Exactly where the enlightened soul goes upon achieving freedom from rebirth is one of the greatest adventures ever imagined and merits a book in itself.)

Definition

Just what do we mean by reincarnation? The answer has two parts: first, a definition of terms, for the words associated with reincarnation tell much about the phenomenon itself. The second part is more fundamental: what is it that reincarnates from one body to another? Is it the soul? The mind? The intellect? Which part of us is the most essential, the part we continue being even after death?

The word *reincarnation* was introduced into the English language in the middle of the nineteenth century. It is composed of five Latin elements: *re-* = "again;" *in-* = "into;" *carn* = "flesh;" *-ate* = "cause or become;" and *-ion* = "process." *Reincarnation,* then, literally means "the process of coming into flesh again."[7] Implied is the notion that there is something to us that is separate from the flesh, or body, that returns after death.

The word *transmigration,* which is often used interchangeably with reincarnation, is considerably older, having been in English usage since the sixteenth century. It also comes from Latin: *trans-* = "across;" *migr-* = "to go or move;" and *-ation* = "process of causing or becoming."[8] *Transmigration* is "the process of moving across, from one to the other." It is used as frequently as "reincarnation" to signify the crossing of the soul from one body to another. Other words used in this way are *rebirth* and even *preexistence,* which carries a slightly different meaning than pointing to prior births. Although there are many other synonyms for reincarnation, in this book we will confine ourselves to these four.

There are several important words that come from the Greek, such as *metempsychosis: meta-* = "later, beyond, changed;" *em-* or *en-* = "into;" *psyche* = "soul;" and *-osis* = "process." To the ancient Greeks, this was "the process by which the soul gets changed after [death] into [a new body]."[9] Related words include *metensomatosis* and *palingenesis*. All refer to reincarnation—the soul's passing from body to body—but are dated.

One should not confuse reincarnation with resurrection, which is defined quite differently. While reincarnation refers to the life force (soul) passing out of the body, resurrection refers to the religious belief that we will one day be raised again, *in the same body*, with the same identity and familial connections that we had during our time on earth. Most Western religions incorporate some notion of resurrection in their beliefs: "in the end, we will live happily ever after, with the loved ones we knew in this life." Reincarnation is also a part of most Western religious traditions, although relegated in large measure to the mystic or esoteric branches of these traditions. In the East, both mainstream and mystical sects espouse the doctrine of reincarnation, although few give credence to the notion of resurrection. The predominant Eastern view is that after death the material body decomposes, its elements again merging with the earth. It is the non-material soul that continues.

What Is It that Reincarnates?

Most people identify with their gross and subtle bodies—the physical form and the mind/intellect that accompanies it. When asked who they are, most people respond with a name, a profession, a description of their religion (i.e., their acquired faith), or their political affiliations. Sometimes they identify with familial connections, their heritage, or their "roots." Others have a more psychological perspective: "I am sensitive; I would never hurt anyone; I am rational and honest, and I have close ties with others who have similar qualities."

Most readers would be able to identify with the personality traits suggested above or their endless variations. And at first it seems appropriate to define ourselves by such words and concepts, at least in a practical, everyday sense. But do we cease to exist if we change our name? If we lose our job? Or if we convert to another religion? If our sense of morals or ethics becomes compromised? In fact, if all the above traits disappear, do we transform into a non-entity? The question remains: Who are we beyond these changeable, material designations?

Plato described existence in this world as *metasy,* "an in-between state." Living beings, to him, were a combination of matter and spirit, a spark of the eternal caught in a web of temporality, a quantum of knowledge drowning in an ocean of ignorance, a blissful entity captured in a world of pain and madness. Most forms of Eastern thought agree with this view. According to ancient India's Vedic literature, for example, living beings are essentially spiritual—creatures who took birth in the world of matter due to a series of complex yet subtle desires. Such embodied souls are called in Sanskrit *tatashtha-shakti.* The word *tata* signifies the coastal zone that divides land from sea. Sometimes the water covers the land, and at other times the water recedes. Living beings in this world are sometimes covered by forgetfulness of their true nature, and sometimes uncovered.

Can anyone prove that we are essentially spiritual, that we are eternal souls temporarily living in a material body? Some people feel that the answer may lie in the way scientists deal with sub-atomic particles: their existence is accepted because of the effects they produce around them. In other words, although certain sub-atomic particles are not actually seen, they are known to exist by the effect they produce. Similarly, the soul's existence may be known by a detailed analysis of material elements. In India, such analysis is known as *Sankhya* philosophy, and it is an ancient but highly exacting science. Others feel that empiric methods of direct perception are insufficient tools for observing subtle phenomena and must be supplemented with more intuitive instruments. In his unpublished essay *Belief in a Future Life,* J. Paul Williams of Mt. Holyoke College ponders the question:

> The fact that we have no direct experience of souls which do not exist apart from the bodies...need not

force us to the conclusion that [the soul] does not exist. The typical reaction of the materialists to this kind of reasoning is an appeal to stick to the known facts. But the materialistic scientist certainly does not limit himself to immediately experienced data. The limits of our experience are so narrow that if we did not permit our thinking to go beyond them, human thought would be puny indeed. Whoever experienced an atom or an electron? The whole conception of the atomic structure is an inference; it is believed because it is consistent with the way in which elements combine, because it explains why under certain conditions peculiar markings appear on photographic plates. Yet we do not accuse the physicist of irrationality when he says that solid matter, such as rock, is really composed of tiny solar systems in which electrons revolve at incredible speeds around protons. Let no one think he has reached perfection in his habits of thought if he accepts inferential logic in physics but rejects it in theology.[10]

Inferred evidence is not exclusive to theological science; it is a basic tool of the hard sciences and a part of our own daily lives. We have never seen the hearts of our loved ones, but we do not doubt that they exist. We have never seen our ancestors, but our existence is proof enough that they, too, once existed. Perhaps the momentous significance of an unseen soul animating our own body makes its existence so much harder to accept than that of a proton. What more shocking discovery could we make than to learn of our own immortality?

Ultimately, whatever our beliefs, *something* separates living beings from inorganic matter. Something is present in life that is absent in death. The physical, chemical components of the body remain in place at death: heart, brain, skeletal structure, and every chemical present in the body during life; but something else, something non-physical, has been lost. Whatever one chooses to call it, this non-physical life force distinguishes a living body from an inert chemical shell.

What do we know about this unique element that pervades the body? We know that classical science rejected it along with religious dogma, at least when referred to as "the soul"; yet we know it has been accepted by religionists throughout history, with few exceptions. In the interest of finding terms acceptable to both classical science and religion, we will speak of "consciousness," for science studies consciousness as at least a potential non-material force within the body, and religionists often accept consciousness as synonymous with, or at least symptomatic of, the soul.

The Symptom of the Soul

Consciousness is the most fundamental part of human experience; nothing is more intimate or more immediate. Every sense impression—such as seeing the words on this page—means something to us because we are conscious. A chair registers no sensory impression; it is not conscious; it has no soul. But I do; I am; I have a soul. Or do I? Do I have a soul or do I have a body? Who am I—the soul or the body?

Ancient scriptural texts, especially those from India, simplify fundamental ontological questions. For example, in certain classical schools dating back to the Vedantic tradition, there is an elementary exercise that runs something like this: Can I be conscious of my body? Can I be conscious of my hand? My legs? My face? My heart? My mind? Yes, I can be conscious of any part of my body, its pleasures, its pains.

Now, can the body be conscious of itself? The immediate answer is no. My body cannot be conscious of itself; rather, *I* am conscious of *my* body. This simple reflection on the nature of consciousness makes it clear that there is a separation between the body and the self, the living being within who is conscious of the body.

To extend this idea, let us admit that we do not really know if the body is conscious of itself. *We do not know because we are not the body.* I cannot really tell if my finger, chest, or brain, for example, are conscious of themselves. Nor can they tell me anything about their (would-be) perceptions because none of them is a self, a personality. They are, at least empirically, unconscious. Therefore, Vedantic texts conclude, consciousness is personality and personality is consciousness.

The Vedic seers draw out various implications from these conclusions, and these, in turn, lead to other simple exercises in understanding: My finger is not a person. Nor is my leg, my nose, my ear, my brain, or my entire body. These accoutrements of the self cannot tell me who I am or who they are, either individually or collectively, because none of them is a self, a personality. None of them possesses self-experience. It is I who experience things, through them and in them. It is concluded, therefore, that they are different than the person in the body who experiences—for that is me, the possessor of consciousness. Modern teachers of Vedanta often point out that the distinction between body and self is even reflected in our language, for the possessive pronoun suggests that *I* am different than *my* body.

We may perceive this difference between the body and the self in everyday experience. Here is an example: if something were to touch my hand, it would not be empirically correct to say that my hand is conscious of that particular stimulation. If I think about it, I will admit that it is I, through my hand and in my hand, by a process of identification, who am conscious of the touch. The ultimate "self," if you will, uses the brain to pick up signals throughout the nervous system and is thus aware of the workings of the body.

It is also through this process of bodily identification that a man or woman is able to say he or she is hungry, for instance, when, as a matter of fact, it is the stomach, not the person, which is demanding food. The concept of being hungry indicates that "I," the self, am conscious of the contractions of my stomach. If, however, my stomach is locally anesthetized, then the process of self-identification with the stomach is temporarily broken, and I cease to be conscious of its contractions. In other words, "I" would no longer feel hungry, although the body, of course, would still require food. The "self" here is actually the brain and its conditional responses to the world around it; the higher "self" is quite aloof from such perceptions and is not ultimately affected by them.

Direct experience, inference, logic, religious faith, and empiric observation all concur: some sort of conscious energy exists within the body. This conscious energy is the thinker of thoughts and feeler of feelings. The body is an instrument; the conscious energy is the player of that instrument. I am no more my brain or nervous system than a guitarist is the guitar he plays. As a musician produces music with a musical instrument, so I—the thinker—produce thoughts with a thinking instrument: the brain.

Moreover, if an instrument is destroyed, the musician is not necessarily destroyed as a consequence. Analogically, if my body is destroyed, I am not necessarily destroyed with it. If my guitar is destroyed, I would have to get another to make music—or I would have to stop playing the guitar altogether. But I exist apart from the guitar, and my longevity does not depend upon the longevity of my instrument. Guitars may come and go, but expert players will live on. This conception is consistent with the First Law of Thermodynamics, or the Law of Conservation of Energy. Basically, this law says that energy cannot be created or destroyed. If it exists, it continues to exist. Likewise, if the "soul" exists at all, as we have seen it does, then it must subsist in sustained existence. As the sages of India have told us: "For the existent there is no cessation, and for the non-existent—like a dream or an illusion—there is no endurance."

Where does the energy within the body go at the time of death? Nature supplies numerous hints that suggest a sensible answer. Consider, for example, the changes of the body we undergo in this one life, from childhood, to youth, to old age—changes that occur while the person remains in the same body. Physiologically, the cells of our bodies constantly deteriorate and die so that after approximately seven years the cellular structure of the body has been completely overhauled. In *The Human Brain*, Professor John Pfeiffer points out that "your body does not contain a single one of the molecules that it contained seven years ago." He compares the living body to a whirlpool. The essential form appears the same, but all the ingredients stream through at a dizzying pace.

In a 70-year lifetime, a person physiologically "dies" and is "reborn" ten times; and while these intermediate "deaths" do not involve reincarnation as such, they allow us the remarkable experience of looking back, in this lifetime, to previous lives: as infants, children, youths, grown-ups. Strictly speaking, these are obviously not previous lifetimes: the evidence available suggests that reincarnation only rarely permits us to carry the recollection of our previous life into our new one. They are, nonetheless, past physical selves that no longer exist. Different bodies, same person—a simple exercize in seeing the difference between the physical and spiritual self, in seeing who we appear to be and who we really are.[11]

And regarding our loss of memory from life to life: there is now a growing body of scientific evidence suggesting there is ample reason for such forgetfulness. It seems that large quantities of oxytocin, one of the hormones of the posterior pituitary gland (which increases the contractions of the uterus during childbirth and prevents subsequent bleeding), produces loss of memory in laboratory animals and causes even well-trained animals to lose their ability to perform otherwise easy tasks. Because a woman's oxytocin floods her child's system during the later stages of pregnancy, it is not unreasonable to suppose that this natural drug flushes away memories of former incarnations along with conscious remembrance of birth.[12] Not that smearing of the slate of memory doesn't occur in life outside the womb. The inability of keen-minded adults to remember their earliest years and the frequent loss of recall among the elderly are, perhaps, nature's way of imparting the relative insignificance of conscious memory. Besides, it is undoubtedly an act of mercy to instill forgetfulness in a soul who takes a new birth: imagine the hardship of trying to live one life while plagued with memories of another. We would hardly be able to develop relationships with new families and friends, and learn our necessary lessons, if forced to recollect those of former incarnations. Prior loves and losses could make new adventures in life appear futile.

Benjamin Walker, in his brilliant book, *Masks of the Soul,* writes convincingly about the subject of reincarnation forgetfulness:

> To this a number of answers have been given. To start with, there is the shattering experience of death in the previous incarnation, which obliterates much of the memory of what has happened to us. Again, in the new life, the mind is prepared for fresh experiences, and the trauma of birth effectively erases much of what came before.
>
> It is also to be remembered that the body, the seat of the sense organs, and the instrument of our involvement with the material world, may be as much a hindrance as a help in our ability to recall the past. Perhaps the remembrance of our earlier life would

enormously complicate our present life. It would cause needless confusion to have to live with the problems of more than one life at a time.

The experiences of each life are part of the process of our education, and having reached a certain level it is not necessary that we should remember the stages by which we reached it. We do not remember the early stumbling efforts by which we learned to walk, talk, read or write. It has also been argued that recollection would hinder probation. The soul's struggle from life to life must be isolated from the distracting influences of its past.[13]

Reincarnation and Western Culture

While ideas about reincarnation are usually associated with great thinkers of the East, the concept also has a long and honored history in Western culture. Renowned historian Sirapie Der Nersessian, for example, tells us that

It is not generally realized to what great extent the ideas of the East had penetrated the Graeco-Latin world: from the time of Alexander, the rise of skepticism had indicated a counter-influence from India.[14]

Der Nersessian tells us that Apollonius, a renowned Pythagorean philosopher from before the time of Christ, travelled from Ephesus to India and brought back to the West many of the secrets of the *brahmanas*.[15] The Greek historian Herodotus (fifth century BC) opined that the Egyptians were the first reincarnationists, but the Egyptians themselves acknowledged the East, and India in particular, as the real source of transmigration thinking.[16] Early Egyptian writings tell how the god Osiris, who personified esoteric knowledge, was driven to Egypt from India in the form of a spotted bull—all followers of Osiris accept that the god reincarnated as the bull. Like early Indian traditions, then, the early Egyptians extended their conception of reincarnation to include even the animal species.[17]

Richard Garbe was perhaps the most well-known Indic scholar of his day (late 19th century), and while he wrote on behalf of Christianity he nonetheless argued that India was the original influence on early Greek [and, consequently, the whole of Western] thought.[18] Indologist/historian Arthur Osborne developed these thoughts further, claiming that basic East-Indian practices, such as holistic medicine, a vegetarian diet and religious mysticism, gradually worked their way into Western philosophy and literature. Osborne and other 19th-century scholars argued that reincarnation received its first hearing in the West through India's influence on Western philosophers and writers.

Martin Nilsson, a contemporary European philosopher, represents a contingent of scholars who propose that reincarnationist ideas could have evolved in Greek thought independently of any associations with the East. Prominent writer/philosopher Herbert Long agrees with Nilsson but acknowledges that there is probably some debt to East-Indian philosophy; Long has devoted many pages to the indigenous-origin theory, stating that while some related ideas may have developed independently, in all likelihood the doctrine of reincarnation, as a mature ontological world view, has its roots in India.[19] In support of this theory, he mentions that reincarnation was part of the Eleusinian Mysteries, which are associated with the 15th-century BC philosophers of Eleusis, a small town fourteen miles west of Athens, who are known to have derived many of their ideas from periodic visits to India. These precursors to classical Greek thought fully supported the reincarnationist viewpoint, and many writers like Long conclude that it is for this reason that the doctrine is so strongly represented in early Greek texts.

Reincarnationist ideas in the West can be traced to the sixth century BC, roughly the time of Orpheus and, a little later, Pythagoras. Socrates, whom we know from the writings of his student Plato (third century BC), explained the meaning of the word "soul" by referring to the Orphic poets,[20] who viewed the body as a prison for the soul serving its jail sentence in the world of matter. Orphism developed into an occult religion and became well-known because of its relationship with the popular god Dionysos, another name commonly associated with reincarnationist thinking.

Pythagoras, too, is intimately tied to early reincarnation doctrine.

Ovid's *Metamorphoses* contains a speech in which Pythagoras fully supports the idea of transmigration. According to Diogenes Laertius of the first century AD, one of Pythagoras's most important biographers, Pythagoras was the first to say that "the soul, bound now in this creature, now in that, thus goes on a round ordained of necessity."[21]

One of the best known references to Pythagoras's belief in reincarnation is found in a statement by Xenophanes:

> And once, they say, passing by when a puppy was being beaten, he pitied it, and spoke as follows: 'Stop! Cease your beating, because this is really the soul of a man who was my friend. I recognized it as I heard it cry aloud.'[22]

Diogenes also records that Pythagoras claimed to be able to recall his former lives. Iamblichus, a biographer from the fourth century AD, adds that Pythagoras went to great pains to help others discover details of their former lives as well.[23]

Two other early Greek philosophers, although not as popular, are also associated with reincarnation: Pindar and Empedocles. Pindar is known as one of Greece's greatest lyrical poets, and, in the first half of the fifth century BC, his poems were a popular source of material on reincarnation. Gordon Kirkwood writes that Pindar was the first of the Greek poets to relate reward after death to justice and moral excellence.[24] Empedocles, who flourished around the same time, emphasized another aspect of transmigration. He taught that the souls of this world were originally gods in a higher realm who fell to the embodied world due to the performance of some inappropriate action. They were condemned, he taught, to a cycle of 30,000 births, in a variety of species, including plants and fish. Eventually, says Empedocles, one is reinstated to one's natural condition in the higher spiritual realm, no more to be reborn.[25]

As we move to the time of Plato (a century or two later), we find the culmination of such thoughts regarding reincarnation. This preeminent Greek philosopher and his teacher, Socrates, were arguably the most important Western advocates of reincarnationist teaching. "The real weight and importance of metempsychosis in the West," states the *Britannica* (11th edition), "is due to its adoption by Plato." The first clear reference to reincarnation in Plato's writings is in the *Meno,* where Socrates articulates and accepts the idea. Later, in the *Phaedo,* the idea is developed more fully, and Socrates goes to great lengths to explain it, saying that the soul is invisible, uncompounded, always the same, and eternal; that the soul is immortal and does not cease to exist after death. Socrates says that one does not really learn new things in this life but, rather, recollects truths from previous lives.[26]

The most famous argument in the *Phaedo* is the argument of opposites, which was well-known in ancient Greek culture. Socrates argued that opposites are all-pervading. We see them everywhere—greater and smaller, better and worse, stronger and weaker, just and unjust, and so on. And opposites arise from each other: a man becomes stronger by becoming less weak, for example. This principle, Socrates argues, must apply to life and death: the dead come from the living and the living from the dead. This conclusion conforms to everyday observation, at least in part, for everyone has observed some form of death, which is the natural outcome of life. Socrates concludes that "becoming alive" is actually "becoming the opposite of dying." Therefore, life comes from death. The doctrine of reincarnation, he says, best facilitates this logical course of the soul. He uses elaborate arguments to support this claim, but they are too lengthy to reproduce here.

Many of the logical arguments for reincarnation found in the *Phaedo* echo the words of the ancient Indian scripture *Bhagavad-gita.* In fact, the teachings are so closely related that it is likely that Plato was aware of the Indian text. This is seen even more clearly in Plato's most famous work, the *Republic,* when he tells the story of Er, who was killed in battle but who "came back" while his body lay on a funeral pyre. Er describes the sojourn of the soul in graphic detail, making it clear that Plato fully accepted the doctrine of reincarnation earlier presented by his celebrated teacher. These ideas are developed more fully in the *Phaedrus* and the *Timaeus,* where Socrates articulates a strong belief in transmigration.

Scholars summarize the Greek philosopher's complex version of the doctrine in ten steps: (1) divine origin of the soul; (2) the soul's fall; (3) duration of a cycle of births; (4) address to souls awaiting reincarnation; (5) inevitability of metempsychosis; (6) possibility of release from the cycle after three virtuous lives; (7) judgment in an underground realm; (8) judgment and condemnation of the wicked; (9)

reward of the pious; and (10) an ordered scale of human lives.[27] In many of these ideas, Plato (writing and expanding upon the views of his teacher) confirmed the influence of earlier philosophers, both from Greece and India. His contribution was to give a rational dimension to reincarnationist thinking so that its truth could be perceived even by those who were vehemently opposed to it.

Plato's primary disciple, Aristotle, however, did not share his teacher's enthusiasm for the idea of reincarnation. Neither did the later schools of Stoicism and Epicureanism, which deemphasized the doctrine's importance. The age of science and materialism brought with it a distinctly "this-world" sensibility that all but did away with the earlier notion of reincarnation. While there was an underlying spiritual premise to both Stoicism and Epicureanism, and even to many of the ideas promulgated by Aristotle (whose early works, such as *Eudemus,* accepted the notion of pre-existence and reincarnation), these ideologies set the stage for the more empiric philosophies that followed. Science and technology, with its short-sighted emphasis on the here-and-now, are much indebted to the path paved by Aristotle.

It should be pointed out that Aristotle, while a brilliant thinker, has been severely castigated by philosophers throughout the centuries for his "separation of ideas," or "logic of categories," theory, which proposes that everything fits into its own neat little compartment: religion is religion, science is science, history is history, and so on. The problem, his critics say, is that reality just doesn't work that way. Categories overlap. Religion interacts with history, and science with religion, and on and on. Aristotle's perspective, in this regard, was the precursor of the now notorious Western world view, wherein the harmonious functioning of various categories of existence simply does not apply. After Aristotle, for example, science was able to develop without the counterbalance of religion, and religion without science, making both categories of existence less effectual and less representative of reality as it actually occurs in the real world. The problems that result from this way of viewing reality are vast, and lest we depart from the central theme of this work, we had best leave the critique of Aristotelian logic to a more qualified author.

It should still be mentioned that with the introduction of science and Aristotelian thinking came a tendency by religionists to compromise their more esoteric convictions in order to retain a degree of power in a rapidly changing world. Christianity, as practiced by the majority of churchgoers today, for example, makes no mention of reincarnation, although, as we shall see later in this book, the notion of transmigration played a central role in early Christian theology. The forms of Christianity widely embraced today were largely molded by the teachings of Thomas Aquinas, who based his entire world view on Aristotelian logic and rejected the more mystical aspects of his own tradition, including the idea of reincarnation. Christians with a predilection for this form of their religion might be interested to learn that the Aristotelian-Thomistic view is counterbalanced by the Platonic-Franciscan traditions which are equally Christian but more sympathetic to a philosophy that includes reincarnation. Both points of view grew up side by side, with supporters and detractors all along the way.

The early Roman Empire, just after the time of Jesus, saw a resurgence in reincarnationist thinking. Plutarch (AD 46-120) wrote authoritatively about the conception of transmigration, as did Porphyry in the third century. Porphyry often quoted the Mithraists as his source of information regarding reincarnation, and this, too, has led scholars to believe that the notion was prevalent among early Christian sects. As we shall see, reincarnation plays a powerful role in each of the world's five major religious traditions—Hinduism, Buddhism, Judaism, Christianity, and Islam—and we will explore these traditions by beginning with the earliest ones and concluding with those that are most recent. Finally, we will survey the plethora of recent scientific evidence suggestive of reinarnation, and we will draw conclusions based upon the obvious implications of that evidence.

ENDNOTES

1 *Gates of Prayer* (New York: Central Conference of American Rabbis, 1975), p. 624.

2 George Gallup, Jr. and William Procter, *Adventures in Immortality* (New York: McGraw-Hill, 1982), pp. 137-8.

3 Walter Martin, *The New Age Cult* (Minneapolis: Bethany House Publishers, 1989), p. 85.

4 Margot Russell, *Reincarnation Today* (London: Pantone Publications, 1989), p. 6.

5 Norman L. Geisler and J. Yutaka Amano, *The Reincarnation Sensation* (Wheaton, Ill.: Tyndale House Publishers, 1986), p. 26.

6 Edward Sykes, *Studies in Biology: Humans and Animals* (New York: Edington Press, 1987), pp. 25-30.

7 John Algeo, *Reincarnation Explored* (Wheaton, Ill.: The Theosophical Publishing House, 1987), pp. 133-4.

8 Ibid.

9 Ibid.

10 J. Paul Williams, *Belief in a Future Life*, in manuscript form.

11 There is an argument that, neurologically, the brain cells are not actually replaced but only undergo "radical change." We see this as begging the question. How many changes constitute replacement? If a cell undergoes change—changing from cell X to cell N—has not cell N actually replaced cell X? The issue remains the same: something animates the neuro- and biological body which "varies not, nor changes in the midst of things that vary and change," as Plato once put it.

12 For more on this, see Joe Fisher, *The Case for Reincarnation* (New York: Bantam Books, 1984), p. 83.

13 See Benjamin Walker, *Masks of the Soul: The Facts Behind Reincarnation* (Northamptonshire: The Aquarian Press, 1981), pp. 88-89.

14 *Larousse Encyclopedia of Byzantine and Medieval Art*, ed., Rene Hughe (New York, 1959), p. 14.

15 Ibid.

16 See Joe Fisher, *The Case for Reincarnation* (New York: Bantam Books, 1984), p. 57.

17 Ibid.

18 See Richard Garbe, *Philosophy of Ancient India* (Chicago: Open Court Publishing Company, 1897), pp. 32-56.

19 Herbert S. Long, *A Study of the Doctrine of Metempsychosis in Greece: From Pythagoras to Plato* (Baltimore: J.H. Furst Company, 1948), pp. 5-9.

20 See Plato, Cratylus 400c.

21 See Diogenes Laertius, *Lives of Eminent Philosophers*, trans., R.D. Hicks, Loeb Classical Library, two volumes (London: William Heinemann, 1925). See 2:333; 8.14.

22 Diogenes Laertius, 8.36.

23 See Iamblichus, *Life of Pythagoras*, trans., Thomas Taylor (London: John M. Watkins, 1818), pp. 30-1.

24 Gordon Kirkwood, ed., *Selections from Pindar*, American Philological Association Textbook Series, no. 7 (Chico, California: Scholars Press, 1982), p. 71.

25 Empedocles, *Purifications*, 146-7. Also noteworthy is that Empedocles regarded the killing of animals, even for the important purpose of eating them, to be sinful, causing rebirth in the lowest of species. This idea was subsequently attributed to Orphic and Pythagorean influences on Empedocles. See *Purifications*, 118-27.

26 *Phaedo*, 69d-72a. See, too, 78b-80c and 105c-106e for elaborate arguments on the eternality of the soul and rebirth.

27 For an elaborate explanation of these philosophical principles and complete reference information showing that Plato utilized the teachings of his predecessors in formulating these ideas, see Bobby Kent Grayson's unpublished Ph.D. dissertation, *Is Reincarnation Compatible with Christianity? A Historical, Biblical, and Theological Evaluation* (Fort Worth, Texas: Southwestern Baptist Theological Seminary, September, 1989), pp. 66-7. Also see Clifford H. Moore, *Ancient Beliefs in the Immortality of the Soul* (New York: Cooper Square Publishers, 1963), pp. 21-36.

Chapter 1

Hinduism

As the embodied soul continually passes, in this body,
from childhood, to youth, to old age,
the soul inhabits another body at the time of death.
—Bhagavad-gita

In India, the ancient holy land of Krishna, Rama, Buddha, and countless *avataras* (incarnations of the divine), reincarnation is a reality as self-evident to the humble street-sweeper as it is to the learned *pandita* (scholar) or the saintly *sadhu* (holy person). Although there is a certain scholastic contingent who claim that the notion of reincarnation is only found in India's later philosophical literature and not in the original scripture called the Veda, there are in fact references to it in the earliest Vedic writings: "He who produced him does not know him. From him who sees him, he is concealed. He is hidden within the womb of his mother. Taking many births, he has entered upon misery."[1] Similar references pervade the *Atharva Veda*, the *Manu-samhita*, the *Upanishads*, the *Vishnu-purana*, the *Bhagavata-purana*, the *Mahabharata*, the *Ramayana*, and the many other texts that are either part of the original Sanskrit Veda or else belong to accepted supplementary Vedic literature. This vast scriptural tradition is the

23

foundation for the Hindu world's unshakeable acceptance of reincarnation, and a few direct examples will make this clear:

> O learned and tolerant soul, after roaming in waters and plants, a person enters the womb and is born again and again. O soul, you are born in the body of plants, in trees, in all created animate objects, and in waters. O soul, blazing like the sun, after cremation, having reached the fire and the earth for rebirth, and residing in the belly of your mother, you are born again. O soul, having reached the womb, again and again, you auspiciously lay in your mother's body, as a child sleeps in her mother's lap. (*Yajur Veda*,12.36-37)

The *Shvetasvatara Upanishad* (5.11) gives further insight into the nature of rebirth:

> As the body is augmented by food and water, so the individual self, augmented by its aspirations, sense contact, visual impressions, and delusion, assumes successive forms in accordance with its actions.

The *Brihadaranyaka Upanishad* (4.4.1-4) goes still further in outlining just how reincarnation occurs:

> [At the time of death] the area of his [the soul's] heart becomes lit and by that light the soul departs either through the eye, the head, or through other apertures of the body. And when he departs, the *pranas* [the various life airs] follow him to his next destination…His knowledge and his deeds follow him, as does his previous wisdom, if not specific details of his former life.
>
> Just as a caterpillar, when it reaches the end of one blade of grass, and after having properly approached another one, draws itself together toward the new blade, so the soul, after having thrown away the prior

body and its ignorance, draws itself together, and latches onto the new body. And as the goldsmith, taking a piece of gold, turns it into another, more beautiful shape, even so does this soul, after having thrown away the old and useless body, makes unto himself newer and, hopefully, better bodies, according to his previous actions, ability and desires.

The law of *karma*, which in this context refers to the creating of a particular next life commensurate with the quality of this one, is implicit in these texts. The verbal root of *karma* is *kri*, "to do," or "to act," a word that implies causality. In other words, it refers to not only action but also its inherent reaction. *Karma* has a negative aspect known as *vikarma*, which can be roughly translated as "bad *karma*." It is "bad" in the sense that it refers to harmful or base activities that lead to rebirth in lower species of life and bind one negatively to the world of birth and death. *Karma* of the preferred sort refers to pious, charitable activities that result in a desireable reaction—materially enhancing but also binding to the material world. Finally, there is a category of action called *akarma;* this refers to spiritually-based activities— activities that do not engender a material reaction. *Akarma* alone frees us from the cycle of birth and death, from reactions both positive and negative that bind us to the world of duality; it frees the soul to return to its original nature. These spiritual activities are of a devotional nature. The scriptures of the world share a common description of such spiritual activities and concur that such conduct is superior to "good" as well as "bad" *karma*, although the Vedic texts offer descriptions embodying the clearest categorical distinctions between the three kinds of activities: good, bad, and transcendent.[2]

Uninformed Westerners often use the word *karma* interchangeably with the word "fate," a concept that comes from the Greek *moira,* an action/reaction philosophy that was considered binding even for the gods. There was no way to rise beyond fate as defined by the Greeks. Greek tragedy, one of the earliest and most popular forms of Western literature, is grounded in *moira,* and is characterized by a sense of helplessness and inevitability. *Karma*, however, can be transcended. Indian literature is, consequently, a stranger to tragedy, for *karma*, unlike *moira,* can be neutralized or even erased through spiritual practices.[3] This is observed by Wendy D. O'Flaherty, Professor of Religion at the University of Chicago:

> ...devotion to God can overcome *karma*. This simple faith has an elaborate, classical foundation in the philosophy of Ramanuja [eleventh century], who maintained that God could ïeven override the power of *karma* to draw repentant sinners to him. Thus the doctrine of *karma* is deeply determined by other important strains of Indian religion in which the individual is able to swim against the current of time and fate.[4]

Hinduism teaches that the mass of people are motivated to act by their perception of what will bring the most immediate rewards. This leads to various social and anti-social behavior, resulting in the mixed enjoyment associated with life in the "highly evolved" human species or suffering rebirth into the multifarious lower species. The rules governing these higher and lower births fill hundreds of volumes of Vedic and post-Vedic texts, but scholars have determined that traditional Indian views on death are of three kinds:

1. **The Early Vedic View**
   This tradition maintains that the householder engaged in materialistic [i.e., sinful] affairs goes immediately after death to the realm of Yamaraja, the nether regions, where his hope for salvation lies in offerings of food and water from his children and grandchildren throughout the generations.[5] After spending an unspecified time in this state, one "dies again" (possibly a reference to the soul's continuing journey toward its next incarnation through various intermediary way-stations) and passes through the various material elements (earth, water, air, fire, ether, and other, more subtle elements as well), eventually being "recycled" through the food chain[6] and finally being born again in one of the 8,400,000 species that pervade the universe.

2. **The Puranic View**
   To this early view, the *Puranas* ("ancient histories") added the

notion of unlimited types of heavens and hells where the dead are rewarded or punished according to their pious or impious actions. The *Puranas* describe that the soul wanders through these subtle spheres of existence before being reborn in another body that will afford the chance to pursue self-realization.

3. The Samsara View

This is the matured Hindu explanation of death, a culmination of the Vedic and Puranic concepts. *Samsara* teaches that, immediately after death, the soul is reborn into the material world and continues the cycle over and over again until achieving purified consciousness free from material desires. At that time, the purified soul returns to the spiritual realm, the spawning ground from which all souls originally come. There, one resumes one's natural, constitutional life in the company of God. Contemporary Hinduism, as well as Vaishnavism, Shaivism, and a host of other popular East-Indian traditions, hold this perspective, seeing it as the essential truth of all previous teachings.

The complexity of these subjects and the immense detail afforded by Vedic texts and commentaries are staggering. Related ideas, such as life in the womb, are explained so completely that the Vedas—by sheer volume of data—are considered by many to be the most authoritative and complete source of information on the subject of reincarnation. To give but one small example, the *Bhagavata-purana*,[7] considered the essence of Indian holy books, offers an elaborate explanation of the development of consciousness from fetus to death:

> Having gone through all the miserable, hellish conditions and having passed in a regular order through the lowest forms of animal life prior to human birth, and having thus been purged of his sins, one is reborn again as a human being on this earth. (3.30.34)

> Under the supervision of the Supreme Lord and according to the results of his work, the living entity, the soul, is made to enter the womb of a woman through the particle of a man's semina to assume a particular kind of body. (3.31.1)

> On the first night, the semina and ovum mix, and on the fifth night the mixture ferments into a bubble. On the tenth night it develops into a form like a plum, and after that it gradually turns into a lump of flesh. (3.31.2)

> In the course of a month, a head is formed, and at the end of two months the hands, feet, and other limbs take shape. By the end of three months, the nails, fingers, toes, body hair, bones, and skin appear, as do the organ of generation and the other apertures in the body, namely the eyes, nostrils, ears, mouth and anus. (3.31.3)

> Within four months from the date of conception, the seven essential ingredients of the body (lymph, blood, flesh, fat, bone, marrow, and semina) come into existence. At the end of five months, hunger and thirst make themselves felt, and at the end of six months, the fetus begins to move in the abdomen—on the right side if the child is a male and on the left side if female. (3.31.4)

Although compiled thousands of years ago by sages, the verifiable portions of this text conform to modern scientific research. The *Bhagavata* goes on to explain that while the womb is a safe, nurturing place for the newly embodied soul, this same soul must also experience various types of pain in the womb, and that the trauma of this experience allows the soul to forget its prior lifetimes. If the soul did not forget, says the *Bhagavata,* it would have far too much baggage, as it were, to carry in this life. Indeed, the soul carries the memories of former lives in its subconscious mind, but externally it forgets so that it can appropriately react to its new set of parents and environment in this lifetime. In the Vedic view, the pain of birth (along with the death of the prior body) is at least partly responsible for the forgetfulness that accompanies each successive birth. Philosophers both East and West have long speculated about this peculiar oblivion, and it has remained a central concern for those who defend reincarnationist theory and no less for those who deny it. "If we have lived before," they ask, "then why don't we remember it?"

Saints and theologians have considered various answers. In the *Pistis Sophia,* Jesus speaks of the soul as drinking from a cup "filled with the water of forgetfulness." This idea is illuminated in the 10th book of Plato's *Republic.* There, we are introduced to the valiant Er, who informs us that each individual has the ability to choose the circumstances of his next incarnation. After they make their choice, Er tells us, they drink from the River Lethe (Greek for "forgetfulness"), and this wipes their memories clean so they can engage in their new life unimpeded. "Body," wrote the Greek philosopher Plotinus, "is the true river of Lethe; for souls plunged into it forget all."[8] As mentioned earlier, modern medicine can also be credited with discovering a possible explanation for the cosmic amnesia of the soul: a hormone called oxytocin, which controls a pregnant woman's rate of labor contractions, also controls our forgetfulness of traumatic events.[9]

However this forgetfulness comes about, the *Bhagavata* tells us that the fetus suffers according to its *karma* in the womb. But because its consciousness is not yet fully developed, it can tolerate the pain and gradually make its appearance in the world. The *Bhagavata* continues:

> The child remains just like a bird in a cage, without freedom of movement. At that time, if the child is fortunate, he can remember all the troubles of his past one hundred births and he grieves wretchedly. (3.31.9)

At this point, the *Bhagavata* imparts, the soul within the fetus remembers its debt to the Lord and prays for forgiveness. He remembers his fall from heavenly existence and transmigration through countless bodies. The repentant soul in the womb expresses an intense desire to be reinstated in the Lord's service. The *Bhagavata* describes the soul's longing for freedom, its thirst to be rid of *maya* (illusory existence) once and for all, and to put an end to its material sojourn. The fetus declares its total disgust for life in the world of matter and concludes its prayer: "Let me remain in this condition [in the womb]; although it is in some ways quite miserable, it is better not to fall a victim to *maya* again by being born—by going outside of the womb and into the world."

However, once born, the *Bhagavata* tells us, the newborn is lulled into a sense of false security by loving parents and relatives, and again falls victim to the illusions of material existence. From childhood, the reincarnated soul exists in a materialistic stupor, absorbed in the play of the senses and the objects of their gratification. The *Bhagavata* elaborates:

> As a sleeping person acts according to the body mani-
> fested in his dreams and accepts it to be himself, so
> one identifies with his present body, which he acquired
> because of his past religious or irreligious actions, and
> is generally unable to know his past or future lives.
> (6.1.49)

The remainder of the massive 31st chapter of the *Bhagavata*'s Third Canto gives a detailed outline of life in the material world, from childhood, to youth, to adulthood, to old age—and then describes how the process starts all over again. This phenomenon is called *samsara-bandha,* or "conditioned life in the cycle of birth and death." The goal of human life, says the *Bhagavata*, is to free oneself from this cycle by the yogic process of devotional love (*bhakti-yoga*), which centers on chanting the holy name of the Lord.

The *Bhagavata* reveals this conclusion to readers only after much philosophical and theological preparation. Using these portions of the *Bhagavata*, the *Upanishads* (108 holy books that offer philosophical analysis of Vedic thought) and *Bhagavad-gita* (the brief but quintes-sential Indian text), scholars and devotees alike have summarized ancient India's process of liberation from *samsara* as a movement through five basic steps to enlightenment.[10]

(1) Each of us is a living soul within a material body. The Vedic texts are precise regarding the soul within the body: "When the upper point of a hair is divided into one hundred parts and again each of such parts is further divided into one hundred parts, each such part is the measurement of the dimension of the spirit soul."[11]

Due to texts such as this, the tradition unanimously teaches that the universe consists of innumerable particles of spiritual atoms—souls—which are measured as one ten-thousandth of the upper portion of the hair. Knowledge of the soul's dimensions is augmented by information regarding the position of the soul in the body:

> The soul is atomic in size and can be perceived by perfect intelligence. This atomic soul is floating in the five kinds of air (*prana, apana, vyana, samana* and *udana*), is situated within the heart, and spreads its influence all over the body of the embodied living entities. When the soul is purified from the contamination of the five kinds of material air, its spiritual influence is exhibited.[12]

The soul is thus caught in the body and falsely identifies with it from the moment of its birth.

In one lifetime we pass through many different bodies—baby, child, youth, adult, and so on—but remain the same person. We do not change; it is our body that changes. The *Bhagavad-gita* describes this first step to enlightenment: "As the embodied soul continually passes, in this body, from boyhood to youth to old age, so the same soul passes into another body at death."[13]   The *Bhagavad-gita* indirectly asks: since the soul has been transmigrating from body to body in this one life, why *assume* that it discontinues this process at the time of death? This 700-verse "Bible" of Hinduism offers the following analogy: "As a person puts on new garments, giving up the old ones, similarly, the soul accepts new material bodies, giving up the old and useless ones."[14] Comparing the body to used clothing is quite appropriate: we buy clothes according to our taste and means; we acquire a new body according to our desire and *karma*—this constitiutes our "means" for establishing future states of existence.

(2) Souls first devolve, then evolve, through the species. The soul, attempting to be the Lord of its own domain, leaves the spiritual realm, where God is supreme, and becomes an angelic being in Brahma's world (which is considered the highest heavenly planet of the mundane sphere). From there, a small quantity of souls may return to their original spiritual state. The majority, however, due to irrational passions associated with the body and envy borne of life in a self-centered world, fall to the lowest species of life, in lower planets, and gradually go through each of the 8,400,000 forms. The Vedic literature describes 8,400,000 species of life: aquatics, plants, insects, reptiles, birds, four-legged beasts, and various kinds of human beings. The soul eventually evolves to the human species, of which there are 400,000 varieties (including civilized, less civilized, godly, residents of upper worlds, and so on). While being born and reborn as humans with various levels of consciousness, the soul learns its lessons and accrues new *karma*. Experience of these many embodied lives is meant to awaken the instinct that life without the Lord is hellish and that our constitutional position involves returning to the Lord's kingdom as His servant. As the *Gita* says, "After many births and deaths, he who is actually in knowledge surrenders unto Me [God], knowing Me to be the cause of all causes and all that is. Such a great soul is very rare."[15]

(3) Actions we perform in this body determine our next body. The Vedic texts assert that the soul's transmigration from body to body does not take place in a random way. If, in a particular lifetime, the soul engages in the lifestyle of a lusty rogue, he will likely be reborn as a dog or wolf. God is merciful, and He fulfills the desires of all living entities. The *Gita* teaches that subtle reality becomes gross reality: if we contemplate the objects of the senses, the fruits of this contemplation will gradually manifest in the external world, and we develop attachment for these mental creations as well as their tangible counterparts. From attachment, lust develops, and by this we sustain our embodied condition and our sojourn through the material world.

Our journey from body to body is instigated and facilitated by our most subtle desires and our *karma*. Again, we may reasonably ask, "Who would desire to be a dog or a wolf?" Ostensibly, no one. But all too often our aspirations are not what we at first think they are or would like them to be. In fact our actions belie our true desires. If we want to spend our lives in the sluggishness of sleep, for example, why would nature not give us the body of a bear, who sleeps months at a time? Or if we are preoccupied with sex, why should we not have the body of a pigeon, which is physically able to have sex hundreds of times in one day?

Each of the 8,400,000 species offers the eternal soul a body that best facilitates a particular type of sense enjoyment. This, according to the Vedas, is God's accommodation for those of His children who seek to live apart from Him in the world of matter: a playground where we can taste all of material nature's delicacies and discover that none equal the ananda ("spiritual bliss") of the kingdom of God.

(4) One must know the two souls that pervade the body. Within each body dwell two souls: the individual spark of life (you, me) and the source of all life (God) in a localized form called Supersoul. The *Bhagavad-gita* says, "Besides the atomic spiritual soul, in this body there is another enjoyer—a transcendental enjoyer—who is the Lord. He is the supreme proprietor, overseer, and permitter, and He is known as the Supersoul (*paramatma*)."[16]

The existence of the Supersoul and atomic soul in the body of each living entity should not be interpreted as polytheism. There are unlimited numbers of atomic souls, say the Vedas, but only one Supersoul. The *Bhagavad-gita* explains: "Although the Supersoul appears to be divided into many, He is not; He is situated as one."[17] The Vedic texts analogize this with the sun and its reflections: there is one sun in the sky, but its reflection will appear simultaneously in thousands of waterpots. Similarly, there is only one God, but He expands Himself as the Supersoul in the hearts of all living creatures and in every atom of creation. Knowing that God lives in our heart (as Supersoul) is prerequisite to breaking free from the cycle of birth and death.

It is important to distinguish between the Supersoul and atomic soul, never confusing the two as one: they are eternally individual and have a loving relationship that surpasses all others. The *Upanishads* compare the soul and the Supersoul to two friendly birds sitting in a tree. The first bird is trying to enjoy the fruits of the tree—an analogy that refers to the living being struggling to obtain material happiness in this world. The second bird (Supersoul) is self-satisfied—He is not here to gain anything for Himself; rather, He acts as well-wisher to His ambitious friend, observing his inevitable successes and failures throughout various lifetimes. He waits for his friend to come to his senses (or, rather, to transcend his material senses) and turn to Him in love and devotion. This will happen as a matter of course, since the soul, in this world, is in an unnatural environment—a fish out of water. Returning to spiritual waters, however, is a process that can take billions of years.

In the Upanishadic analogy, the two birds are specifically

described as two *green* birds in a *green* tree, and so it is easy to confuse one for the other. Contemporary Indian philosophy in general, and the doctrine of Shankaracharya in particular, has done much to confuse the two birds, teaching that God and the living entity are in fact one. However, actual Vedic philosophy, especially as preserved in the genuine Vaishnava lineages, rejects the idea of existential homogeneity and, instead, emphasizes the difference between the living being and his Maker.

(5) The soul can escape rebirth by cultivating consciousness of God. The Supersoul is the dearest friend of the living being—watching him, guiding him, and eventually sending him a genuine *guru* who can teach him the intricacies of spiritual life. Studying scripture in the association of other aspiring devotees, under the guidance of a qualified preceptor, is the fundamental Vedic program for enlightenment. The results of such an applied study are: *ruchi* (the taste for spiritual life); *vairagya* (the sense of detachment necessary to sustain spiritual practices); and eventually *prema* (love of God), which guarantees freedom from repeated birth and death.[18]

One thus situated in transcendence no longer hankers or laments for anything, but lives in this world simply in service to God. Such sainthood brings with it untold bliss, for one is only officially, or externally, still in the realm of matter. In actuality, that person resides in the spiritual kingdom with God. Indian texts describe such pure devotees as being in full knowledge, as experiencing eternality and the highest pleasure that comes from love of God. Such notables have unlimited compassion for less evolved souls and devote their lives to helping them acquire a similar state of spiritual consciousness. With this single-minded determination to work on the Lord's behalf, they are freed from the reaction to all *karma*, and at the end of this life, do not return to this world but, instead, go to be with the Lord of the heart.

Concluding Thoughts

The Vedic texts of ancient India are perhaps the most thorough and time-honored of all literatures dealing with the subject of reincarnation. The systematic literature of the Vedic sages and the detailed analysis of rebirth and the various levels of existence found therein are just now being explored by Sanskritists, Indologists, and historians of religion. As the Western world learns these esoteric secrets, we may well find long-forgotten truths about our own culture, about our own religious traditions. And as we delve deeply into the ideas left us by self-realized Vedic teachers, our collective consciousness may evolve to a more spiritual level, with healing effects, and may serve as the panacea we have searched for throughout the annals of recorded history.

Our consciousness is naturally most absorbed in that which is dearest to us. "And whatever state of being one remembers when he quits his body," the *Gita* tells us,[19] "that state he will attain without fail." The character of the subtle body (the mind, intelligence, and the sense of identity) at the time of death is determined by the sum total of activities during one's lifetime. If a human being is taught to change his subtle body by focusing on God, at the time of death his subtle body will create a gross body in which he will be a devotee of the Lord—or, if he is still more advanced, he will not take another material body at all but, as we have noted, will immediately get a spiritual body and thus return to the original, spiritual home, back to Godhead.

All of this is nicely summarized by Dr. Guy L. Beck:

> According to the texts, Yoga, variously defined but almost always involving mental purification, combined with Bhakti, devotion toward a Personal Deity, is thus the remedy for the pains and ills of the innumerable births in the cycle of transmigration. In fact, it is solely through the agency of a Personal Deity (whether Vishnu, Krishna, Rama, Shiva, or the Goddess), who acts as a kind of deus ex machina, that one is freed from the horrors of transmigration and released into permanent beatitude. Though the religious of these groups do not pretend to achieve the Vedic heaven per se, the permanent spiritual afterlife outlined in the Bhakti scriptures can be seen as a further development, perhaps a more direct answer to the basic need of all humankind for emancipation from

what the German philosopher Nietzsche termed, "the eternal recurrence of the same."[20]

Beck's admiration of the Hindu tradition is heartening, especially in his well-researched conclusion that the various forms of Indian philosophy, in all their diversity, boast the most consistent and well-thought-out doctrine of rebirth the world has ever seen:

> The Hindu doctrine of transmigration, when viewed in comparison with other religious systems and theodicies, is without doubt one of the most complex in the history of the world. Several reasons for this can be tendered: it has endured the pressures of centuries of foreign invasion and political turmoil; it has been responsive to an almost infinite variety of criticism and interpretation both from within and without; it has been molded to conform with many types of religious persuasions, whether monistic, dualistic, monotheistic, polytheistic, non-theistic, etc. Despite this great complexity, however, the doctrine of transmigration, along with the belief in Karma, remains as one of the most pervasive common denominators—regardless of social status, caste, creed, age, gender—among the wide diversity of sects, subsects, philosophical schools, and lay assumptions informing the entire Indian tradition.[21]

ENDNOTES

1 For details on the implications of this *Rig Veda* verse, see S.E. Gopala Charlu, "The Indian Doctrine of Reincarnation," in *The Theosophist,* May, 1892, p. 480.

2 Details on karma can be found in His Divine Grace A.C. Bhaktivedanta Swami Prabhupada, *The Laws of Nature: An Infallible Justice* (Los Angeles: Bhaktivedanta Book Trust, 1991) and *A Second Chance: The Story of a Near-Death Experience* (Los Angeles: Bhaktivedanta Book Trust, 1991). Also see Wendy D. O'Flaherty, ed., *Karma and Rebirth in Classical Indian Traditions*

(Berkeley: University of California Press, 1980) and Ronald W. Neufeldt, ed., *Karma and Rebirth: Post-Classical Developments* (Albany: State University of New York Press, 1986).

3 Klaus K. Klostermaier, *A Survey of Hinduism* (New York: State University of New York Press, 1989), p. 205.

4 Wendy D. O'Flaherty, *The Origins of Evil in Hindu Mythology* (Los Angeles: University of California Press, 1976), p. 16.

5 A painless journey to Yamaloka depends on the successful performance of the *sapindikarana* ceremony by the departed person's son. This consists of a complex series of rituals wherein the *pinda* (a ball of rice) is offered to the deceased parent, allowing him entry into the association of his ancestors. Until that time (either twelve days or twelve months after death, depending upon which texts one refers to), the soul remains in a subtle ghostly form, and only this *pinda-pradana* (also known as the *shraddha* ceremony) permits the departed to enter the next stage of existence.

6 This peculiar early Vedic view of transmigrating through the food chain is expressed by A.C. Bhaktivedanta Swami Prabhupada as follows:
In the process of sacrifice [delineated in the Vedas], the living entity makes specific sacrifices to attain specific heavenly planets and consequently reaches them. When the merit of sacrifice is exhausted, then the living entity descends to earth in the form of rain, then takes on the form of grains, and the grains are eaten by man and transformed into semen, which impregnates a woman, and thus the living entity once again attains the human form to perform sacrifice and so repeat the same cycle. In this way, the living entity perpetually comes and goes on the material path. The Krishna conscious person, however, avoids such sacrifices. He takes directly to Krishna consciousness and thereby prepares himself to return to Godhead. [See *Bhagavad-gita As It Is* (Los Angeles, Bhaktivedanta Book Trust, 1974, reprint) Chapter eight, Text three, p. 413]

7 See His Divine Grace A.C. Bhaktivedanta Swami Prabhupada, trans., Srimad Bhagavatam, Canto three, Chapters thirty and thirty-one (Los Angeles: Bhaktivedanta Book Trust, 1974).

8 Quoted in Joe Fisher, *The Case for Reincarnation* (New York: Bantam Books, 1984), p. 83.

9 Ibid., p. 84. "Research studies have established that large quantities of

oxytocin produce loss of memory in laboratory animals and cause even well-trained animals to lose their ability to perform known tasks. Because a woman's oxytocin floods her child's system, it is not unreasonable to suppose that this natural drug flushes away memories of former incarnations along with conscious remembrance of birth. Not that smearing of the slate of memory doesn't occur in life outside the womb. The inability of keen-minded adults to remember their earliest years and the frequent loss of recall among the elderly is, perhaps, nature's way of imparting the relative insignificance of conscious memory."

10 See Mandaleswara dasa, "Six Lessons on Transmigration," in *Back to Godhead* magazine, Vol. 12, No. 10 (Los Angeles: Bhaktivedanta Book Trust, 1977), pp. 18-23.

11 *Shvetashvatara Upanishad*, 5.9.

12 *Mundaka Upanishad*, 3.1.9.

13 - 17 *Bhagavad-gita*: 2.13; 2.22; 7.19; 13.23; 13.17.

18 As there are many forms of Hinduism, there are many variations of this formula for enlightenment. We have focused on the Gaudiya Vaishnava point of view as representative of the general Hindu perspective, with prema, or "love of God," as the ultimate goal. Traditionally, however, the conception of *purushartha*—material religiosity, economic development, sense gratification, and, at the end, the attempt to become one with the Supreme ("liberation")—is perhaps more commonly understood as the goal of life in normative Hinduism. However, "liberation" (*moksha*) on this path does not necessarily guarantee freedom from birth and death. Even if one merges with the Supreme, one is likely to fall down, since such a merger is an unnatural condition for the living being who is constitutionally connected to the Lord in a relationship of love and service.

19 *Bhagavad-gita,* 8.6.

20 See Guy L. Beck, "Recycling the Atman: Reflections on the Doctrine of Transmigration in Classical Hinduism," in *Concepts in Transmigration*, ed. Steven J. Kaplan (Lewiston, New York: Edwin Mellen Press, 1996), pp. 87-117.

21 Ibid.

Chapter 2

B_{uddhism}

The Books say well, each one's life
The outcome of his former living is;
The bygone wrongs bring forth sorrows and woes
The bygone right breeds bliss.

—Buddha, traditional poem

Buddhism arose in India 2,500 years ago as a reaction to a fanatical priestly class (brahmanism) who saw in Vedic texts an exhortation to animal sacrifice. The path of the Buddha (from the Sanskrit *budh*, or "enlightened") was therefore viewed as a heterodox tradition, although it shares much in common with its parent faith, Hinduism, including its own Buddhistic interpretation of reincarnation. Buddhism, in fact, came to *emphasize* the teaching of "rebirth,"[1] which holds, according to early Buddhist thinkers, that one's primary thought at the time of death becomes the very image that infuses the core of one's new existence in a subsequent body. This reincarnationist view, of course, is borrowed from earlier Hindu teachings.

Unfortunately, there is debate and confusion about what the Buddha himself actually taught regarding the soul and reincarnation, and there are those who opine that he denied the validity of these

39

concepts altogether. This latter view is attributable, at least in part, to the particular variety of Buddhism called Theravada, a South Indian school of thought that teaches that the living being has no eternal soul (*anatman*), and that, consequently, there is no "self" to be reborn. What is called the "self" according to the Theravada school is a transitory combination of five elements (*skandhas*): matter, bodily sensations, perceptions, impulses and emotions, and consciousness. Although Theravada Buddhists admit that the individual is more than a combination of these elements at any particular time, they are quick to point out that at death the five elements disperse and the "self" ceases to exist.

Even the most conservative Theravada Buddhist, however, accepts that the "dissolution" of the individual at death is not a total end to life but rather the beginning of a new phase of existence. A subtle karmic quality that engulfs the "five elements" is said to pass into a fresh body, drawing together a new set of *skandhas* that serve to situate one in a "new life" with new life experiences. There are even texts indicating that "the karma of the five elements" passes in the form of "a germ of consciousness" (*vinnana*) to the womb of a mother[2]—which can be seen as at least a thinly veiled reincarnationist notion.

The Theravada "no-soul" doctrine is said to have originated while the Buddha himself walked the earth, but even at that time it was seen as an unconventional idea that could not be adequately supported by the textual tradition. Research into early Buddhist texts, in fact, reveals that the Theravada view was hardly representative of original Indian Buddhism; in some respects it was even contrary to early Buddhist teaching. And yet there were early Buddhists who held the no-soul perspective to be true: this could explain why even in the East there is much contention over just what the Buddha taught in regard to the soul and reincarnation. A close study, however, reveals in no uncertain terms the Buddha's reaction to the no-soul doctrine:

> And I, O monks, am accused wrongly, vainly, falsely, and inappropriately by some ascetics and Brahmanas: "A denier is the ascetic Gotama, he teaches the destruction, annihilation, and perishing of the being that now exists." These ascetics accuse me of being what I am not, O monks, and of saying what I do not say.[3]

The idea of rebirth is implicit in Buddhism: the enlightened state (*buddhi*), say the Buddhists, cannot be achieved in one lifetime but takes many thousands of years. Buddhist scholar Edward Conze writes: "The state of a Buddha is one of the highest possible perfection. It seems self-evident to Buddhists that an enormous amount of preparation over many lives is needed to reach it."[4] From Buddhism's inception, it acknowledged the existence of the soul and the process of rebirth, even though detractors wrongly accused the Buddha of teaching otherwise. One school of thought has it that early Buddhists, reacting to Hindu orthodoxy, concocted the no-soul doctrine, hoping to establish Buddhism as a tradition theologically distinct from Hinduism. This pride in their philosophical autonomy was prominent among early Buddhists, who were just beginning to wean their religion from its Hindu parentage.

Historians differ on whether the Buddha denied the soul altogether or merely believed in a soul at variance with Hindu definitions. The texts themselves clear up much of the mystery, if read with an understanding of the Buddha's overall teaching, separate from any politically-motivated interpretations. For example, a look at the four Noble Truths—the foundation of Buddhistic thought, which focuses on the inherent desire and consequential suffering of material existence—points squarely to the laws of karma and rebirth.[5] Early Buddhism taught that a living entity may be born into one of five levels of existence: the inhabitants of hell, brute creatures, ghosts, human beings, or heavenly beings. As in conventional Hinduism, desire and karma determine the selection, and the process continues repeatedly until one either "dissolves" at the time of death or else attains Buddhahood and enters *shunyata,* "the great void."[6] Only a few determined aspirants achieve this perfection. For most, the disciplines are too severe and the pleasures of this world too seductive. The result is that most living beings devolve into animal species. Therefore, say Buddhists, other species far outnumber humans. This connects the idea of reincarnation with the suffering that pervades all levels of existence, i.e., the four Noble Truths.

In an article entitled "Buddhism Teaches Rebirth," Christmas Humphreys, one of the Western world's greatest authorities on Buddhist thought, cites the famous list of "ten things which Gotama the Buddha would not have taught"—a list originally compiled by

Mrs. Rhys Davids, a leading Pali scholar of the nineteenth century. In this list, Mrs. Davids clearly states that the Buddha would "never have denied the existence of the real self, the spirit, the soul."[7] Although she was a lifelong student of Theravada Buddhism—which, again, teaches the no-soul doctrine—she adamantly maintained that "Buddha began his mission by advising men to seek thoroughly for the *atman* ("the self"), and ended by bidding men live as having *atman* for their lamp and refuge." The Buddha's concern, she said, was for the actual person—the inner self—on "The Path." And this was a long, hard road, she insisted, which the Buddha knew well would take many lives, and he made this clear in parables and in teachings to intimate disciples.

> If the Buddha…taught [the truth of] *Atta* [self], as [did] his brilliant predecessors in the field of Indian thought, what did he say was Not-self, *an-atta*? He is quite specific. It is the five *skandhas,* the constituents of personality, in which there is no permanent self to be found.…But the monks would not leave this statement alone. Attacking the concept of *atman* as [it had] degraded in the Buddha's day to "a thing"…they swung too far [in the other direction]. "No self, no self" they cried, and in time produced the joyless, cramping doctrine [that is] drearily proclaimed today.

The result of this extreme reaction to brahmanical literalism, of course, is now seen in much of later Buddhism, especially the Theravada school, where, as we have seen, the soul is rejected as a real, separate entity.

Humphreys takes exception to the no-soul perspective. He agrees with the Theravada *bhikkhus* (monks) when they deny materialistic conceptions of the soul; but he insists that the eternal self, when properly understood, is integral to Buddhist thought, and so he asserts that "the *bhikkhus* ignore the 'unborn, unoriginated [self]'…of their own scriptures, as inherent in every manifested thing. Clearly the phenomenal self, whether called ego, shadow, or the evolving soul, is changing all the time." Humphreys concludes that the *bhikkhus* are incorrect when they say, "no soul, no soul, no self at all."[8]

Further evidence of belief in reincarnation is found in *The Jataka Tales* ("Birth Stories") which, according to tradition, were originally told by the Buddha himself—547 stories of the Enlightened One's past incarnations. Often allegorical in style, these narratives delineate the Buddha's sojourn in various species and describe how one can attain Buddhahood by adhering to the principles embodied by the stories. The tales recount how the Buddha incarnated as a *deva,* as an animal, even as a tree in order to help souls in various conditioned states reach liberation; such was his compassion. A well-known *maha-kavya* ("great saying") of Buddhist tradition declares: "There exists not a particle of earth where the Buddha has not sacrificed his life for the sake of creatures." In one *Jataka* tale he incarnates as an elephant and makes great sacrifices for a woman, chiefly by filing off his tusks for her. Remembering his selflessness in that birth, she, in her next life, becomes his disciple and, gradually, a great saint. Reincarnation plays a central role in nearly all 547 *Jataka* tales.

Northern Buddhism

So far we have dealt mainly with southern Buddhism, which is the Buddhism of Burma, Sri Lanka, Cambodia, Thailand, and parts of Vietnam. We have briefly discussed its doctrine of no-soul and offered refutations based on early Indian sources. Now we will explore aspects of northern Buddhism, the Mahayana tradition, found in Tibet, China, Japan, and Korea. This school is much more sympathetic to reincarnation (perhaps because it is more indebted to original Indian Buddhism), which is particularly apparent in the Tibetan form of the religion, where the doctrine of rebirth remains a central teaching.

When the Dalai Lama—the pre-eminent representative of Tibetan Buddhism—visited the United States in 1981, he said, "According to the Theravada school of thought, when a person reaches Nirvana then there is no more person, he completely disappears, but according to *the higher school of thought* the person still remains, the being itself still remains."9

Tibet was originally known as Ti-Boutta—*Ti,* in Chinese, means "deity," and *Boutta,* which comes from the Sanskrit *buddha,* means "wisdom." So Tibet is known as the Land of the Wisdom Deity or the

Incarnations of Wisdom, referring to the successive incarnations of the two highest Lamas, the Dalai and the Panchen. Only the highest monks are called Lamas, accepted throughout the Buddhist community as highly evolved souls who incarnate again and again to help others attain enlightenment. Because of belief in this reincarnation cycle, birthdays are considered unimportant in Tibet, even for Lamas themselves. This is because a birthday is not seen as something unique but rather as something each of us experiences millions of times:

> For the people the date of their king's birth [the Dalai Lama] is quite without interest. He represents in his person the return to earth of Chenrezi, the god of grace, one of the thousand living Buddhas who have renounced Nirvana in order to help mankind...[10]

Northern forms of Buddhism reveal their reincarnationist aspect in other ways, although at times direct reference to rebirth may be somewhat obscure. Chinese Buddhism, for example, is often described as "this-worldly," neglecting reincarnation and similar "abstractions" in favor of more tangible things, such as the beauty of nature. This influence comes largely from China's indigenous teachers, such as Lao Tze and Confucius, whose earliest followers (dating back to the T'ang Dynasty, early in the Christian Era) emphasized the importance of the "natural world" and the beauty of the here-and-now. However, as far as authentic Chinese Buddhism is concerned, there is an ancient scripture known as the *Prajna Paramita Sutra*, written on wooden blocks, which, according to tradition, contain the Buddha's own words. (The Chinese, it is said, were the first to write them down.) Encoded on these greatly revered blocks are esoteric truths that directly point to reincarnation. Buddhists who support the doctrine of rebirth regard these scriptures highly, not only because they are clear about the validity of reincarnationist teachings but because they reputedly contain the Buddha's own words.

Among other early proponents of reincarnation in Buddhist thought is Vatsiputriya,[11] a brahmin who originally belonged to the Sthavira sect. Only 250 years after Buddha, this monk founded the Pudgalavada sect, which was specifically designed to battle the growing conception of Buddhism as a tradition that rejected the doctrine of rebirth. Vatsiputriya faced intense opposition, and his group of stalwart Buddhist monks were renounced as heterodox, giving way to more and more groups who eschewed the doctrine of rebirth.

Zen Buddhism

Zen[12] teachers have traditionally taught reincarnationist ideas, but Zen's focus is on complex meditational techniques and not on metaphysical questions per se, such as those involving reincarnation. Nonetheless, there have been several great Zen masters who taught rebirth and the eternality of the soul. It was clear to these Zen masters that the living being was eternal and did not dissolve when the body ceased to be useful. The great teacher Chao-chou (778-897), for example, wrote, "Before the existence of the world, the Self-nature is. After the destruction of the world, the Self-nature remains intact."[13]

Hui-neng (638-713), whom Zen historians have called "the sixth Chinese patriarch of Zen," once asked his disciples to surround him as he was planning to die. When they heard his intentions, they wept piteously. "For whom are you crying?" the master asked. "Are you worrying about me because you think that I do not know where I am going? If I did not know, I would not leave you in this way. What you are really crying about is that *you* do not know where I am going. If you actually knew, you could not possibly cry, because True-nature is without birth or death, without going or coming. . . ."[14]

By the 13th century, the master Dogen (1200-1253) founded the school of Soto Zen, and expounded reincarnationist ideas more clearly than any previous school of Zen Buddhism. In his essay *Shoji* (the Japanese term for *samsara,* the cycle of birth and death), Dogen analyzes the birth/death/rebirth philosophy of his Hindu and Buddhist predecessors, and establishes its importance for orthodox practitioners of Zen.

Like many other offshoots of Mahayana Buddhism, Zen prescribes an analytical study of death as well as daily meditation. The objective of these practices is to conquer the fear of death and the illusions that come from identifying with the body. From the Buddhist perspective, a typical illusion for the conditioned soul is that death is avoidable in some material sense. One does not overtly think in this way, but lives as if death will never come. Day after day, people enjoy and suffer, with little thought of their inevitable mortality. Buddhist teachers go to great lengths to break their disciples free of material illusion and set them straight about the nature of the body: it must die, even if the essential self lives on. Zen Buddhism teaches that material existence, with its implicit illusion of ongoing bodily enjoyment, is a central obstacle for one who wants to attain enlightenment, and that one must face the reality of death, confronting it with full consciousness.

The Buddhist scholar Buddhaghosh (*circa* fifth century C.E.) was the first to systematize the death meditations of the Buddhists. In one of his most important works, *Visuddhimagga* ("The Path of Purity"), he divided these death meditations into two categories: (1) meditations on the inevitability of death and (2) meditation on the foulness of corpses. Buddhaghosh developed these meditations, centering around the repetition of mantras, into a complex system of eight stages: (1) Death is an executioner holding an axe over the head of every living being; (2) Death is the ruination of all success: all accomplishments are like sand running through the fingers of time, insubstantial, ephemeral; (3) More personally, how will death affect me? What will it feel like? (4) External agents attack the body: germs, parasites, diseases, snakes, animals, people, friends, loved ones—all are potentially dangerous and can cause my death; (5) There is a delicate balance that sustains life, which includes breathing, the mechanics of the body, nutrition, and at any time something could go wrong; (6) Death is waiting for an opportune moment, a frightening adversary who can attack at any time; (7) Human life is brief: at most I have only a few more years to live; (8) I am dying at every moment . . . with each fleeting second, my life is fading away and cannot be retrieved.

Meditation on the foulness of corpses was meant to jolt the practitioner into a heightened awareness of his mortality and prepare him to face death with grace. If one could truly visualize the "rotting, repulsive nature of the body," says Buddhaghosh, and acknowledge that the body is destined to decay and decompose, then one would abandon attachment for it and delve deeply into the pursuit of *atman,* the true self who exists within and transcends the body. The whole idea was to learn how to distinguish between the body and the real self. Death meditations, while sobering, were not a morbid exercise but, rather, a cerebral jolt aimed at freeing the meditator from the bodily concept of life. Only then could one have the calmness of mind necessary to meditate on higher truths. The death meditations were a first step toward focusing the consciousness on that crucial final moment when the soul passes from one body to another. Buddhaghosh asserted that without coming to this point, the whole process of death meditation was a hopeless waste of time.

The idea of rebirth in Mahayana Buddhism is symbolized in its emblematic Bhava Chakra—the Wheel of the Law—depicted as a beautiful fresco in the Tashi'ding monastery in Sikkim.[15] The wheel is divided into six compartments representing the six states of being. The upper portion of the wheel is divided into three: the first are the *lokas,* the highest abode of the gods; the second, the abode of the demigods; and the third, the abode of humankind. The lower three compartments represent the state of animals, the dwelling of ghostly beings, and *naraka,* or hellish existence. Mahayana Buddhism holds that after death, the living being transmigrates, according to its pious or impious acts, into one of these six compartments. If virtuous, the soul may go to the abode of the gods, where it enjoys heavenly pleasures until its good karma has run out. If evil, the soul goes to *naraka,* where it will stay for a time commensurate with its demerits. If one lives an average life of virtue and sin, one is immediately reborn as a human.

Northern Buddhism teaches that one can only attain the ultimate state of enlightenment while in the human form. Nirvana, the supreme state in Buddhistic thought, is not represented by any form within the precincts of the wheel, but is shown by two figures outside the wheel. The personalities who have the virtue of true Nirvana have no place in the wheel of transmigration; they transcend it. However, a small figure of the Buddha can be noticed in each of the six parts of the wheel; this represents his manifestation as the Bodhisattva of Compassion, who takes birth in the world of matter to enlighten others, in all spheres of life, and bring them to perfection.

It is important to note that the entire wheel with its six parts represents the illusion of material life. The condition of being a god, a human, a beast, or whatever, is merely part of the same illusion of bodily existence. The only absolute reality is Buddhahood, which transcends the ordinary world of three dimensions. Because of the very axis of the wheel of illusion, however, which is composed of three creatures representing stupidity, anger and lust, all species of life are bound to fall short of true Buddhahood. Until these three creatures are defeated, one remains the victim of ego and bodily identification and transmigrates through the six compartments of illusory existence.

Around the edge of the Bhava Chakra are twelve secondary compartments called the *nidanas,* which are the twelve states of existence from birth to rebirth. These twelve are arranged on the Chakra like the hours of a clock. It is cyclical, like the wheel of birth and death itself. However, the concentric circles bring one closer and closer to the center, to Nirvana, to Buddhahood, and so, with each birth, one learns and grows. Buddhism, then, while teaching the doctrine of rebirth, is a hopeful philosophy of life, pointing to the ever-flowing progression of existence, wherein one ultimately breaks free and swims in the immortal nectar of reality.

Concluding Thoughts

In the recently published *Concepts in Transmigration,*[16] Professor P.D. Premasiri argues that Theravada Buddhism, contrary to popular belief, embraces reincarnationist doctrine as a necessary one. He writes that the idea of rebirth is as important to this tradition as is "the belief in God in monotheistic religions."[17] He brilliantly reconctructs the history of the doctrine in Theravada Buddhism, citing orthodox sources, such as the Pali *Suttapitaka,* the *Milindapanha,* the treatises of Abhidhamma, Buddhaghosh, and so on. In a methodical manner he seeks to resolve the obvious question: if there is no self in Theravada Buddhist thought, then who or what gets reborn? After a detailed anaysis, he posits the idea of the soul and reincarnation as implicit factors, or constituents, of Buddhist doctrine, thus putting to rest the mistaken notion that transmigration plays no part in Theravada Buddhism.

The same volume includes Professor Richard Pilgrim's essay on East Asian Mahayana Buddhism.[18] And while, from this article, it is obvious that all forms of Mahayana would support reincarnationist thinking, Pilgrim makes an interesting point regarding the Theravada tradition: he contends that from the Mahayana perspective, the

Theravada understanding of rebirth is too literal, too linear. Perhaps it was fear of such literalistic interpretations of the *atma* that led early Theravada Buddhists to reject the soul and rebirth, to throw the baby out with the rice water, as it were. Whatever the case, the recent essays (referred to above) by prominent Buddhist scholars such as Premasiri and Pilgrim bear testimony to the fact that reincarnation is alive and well in Buddhist thought. For anyone who doubts this, we conclude with an ancient Buddhist text, accepted by all orthodox Buddhist theologians today:

> With His divine eye, perfectly pure and surpassing the human, the Bodhisattva saw sentient beings passing away and being reborn, in good castes and bad castes, good destinies and ill destinies, low and high. He distinguished sentient beings migrating according to their karma: "Alas! These sentient beings have misconduct of body, they have misconduct of speech and mind, they belittle the Aryas and hold perverse views. Because of incurring karma with perverse views, when their bodies are destroyed, after death, they are reborn in loss, ill destiny and ruin, in the hells. But these sentient beings have good conduct of body, have good conduct of speech and mind, do not belittle the Aryas, and hold right views. Because of incurring karma with right views, when their bodies are destroyed, they are reborn in a good destiny, in the heavenly worlds."[19]

ENDNOTES

1 The Pali word used by most Buddhists is *punabbhava*, which literally means "an existence again."

2 *Digha-nikaya* 2.63; also see *Samyutta-nikaya* 12.12.3.

3 Quoted in George Grimm, *The Doctrine of the Buddha* (Berlin: Akademie-Verlag, 1958), p. 5.

4 See *Buddhist Scriptures*, trans., Edward Conze (New York: Penguin Classics, 1959), p. 19-20.

5 Concisely, the Truths are as follows: (1) *Dukkha,* or suffering, exists and is all-pervasive; (2) related to this is the truth of the origin of suffering; (3) the truth of the way leading to the end of suffering; (4) What this means in the way of further explanation: all life and action (karma) in this world is ultimately suffering because all pleasure and happiness must come to an end; this suffering has as its basis craving, greed, and all forms of desire (*tanha* or *trishna*); if we could extinguish this desire then all suffering would end and we would attain enlightenment; and The Noble Eightfold Path is the surest means to attain this goal.

The Eightfold Path: man should cultivate right understanding; right motivation; right speech; right conduct; right means of livelihood; right effort (directed toward inner growth); right meditation; and control over the mind. Following this path successfully allows one to achieve enlightenment in the Middle Way—between excessive worldliness and excessive renunciation. Buddhism teaches that this is the way to attain enlightenment (*buddhi*), extinguish suffering (*nirvana*) and attain liberation (*moksha*) from *samsara,* the wheel of rebirth.

6 *Shunyata,* like *nirvana,* is an elusive concept, although there has been a good deal of effort at definition by latter-day Buddhist philosophers. A thoroughly enlightened person, at the time of death, was said to have attained *parinirvana,* the ultimate realization, which was described as a type of "deathlessness." This supreme level of Buddhist accomplishment could not be adequately described because it transcended time, space, birth, death, and all conventional aspects of mundane existence. Most Buddhist texts simply describe *parinirvana* as a state that is beyond any known level of sense perception, a point at which one is said to achieve *shunyata.*

7 From "Things he will not have taught." From *A Volume of Indian and Iranian Studies*, presented to Sir E. Denison Ross (London, 1940). Quoted in Joseph Head and S.L. Cranston, *Reincarnation: The Phoenix Fire Mystery* (New York: Warner Books, 1977), p. 63, an invaluable resource from which much of this chapter is derived.

8 See Christmas Humphreys, "Fifty Years," in *The Middle Way* (August, 1969), p. 51. Also, the Buddha tells his ascetic followers in Undana (8.3), one of the earliest Pali scriptures: "There is a not-born, a not-become, a not-made, a not-compounded. Monks, if that unborn, not-become, not-made, not-compounded were not, there would be apparent no escape from this here that is born, become, made, compounded." [From *The Minor Anthologies of the Pali Canon*, trans., F.L. Woodward (London: Oxford University Press, 1948), p. 98.]

9 Taped lecture, "The Buddha Nature," by the Dalai Lama (July 21, 1981). Available at the Theosophical Society, Wheaton, Illinois. Quoted in Sylvia Cranston and Carey Williams, *Reincarnation: A New Horizon in Science, Religion, and Society* (New York: Julian Press, 1984), p. 240.

10 Heinrich Harrer, *Seven Years in Tibet* (New York: Dutton, 1954), pp. 291-293. There is an alternative tradition which says that the successive incarnations of the Dalai Lama are manifestations of Avalokiteshvara, the Bodhisattva of Compassion. In either case, all schools of Buddhists accept that the Dalai Lama is the same soul reincarnating repeatedly for the benefit of others.

11 See *The Shambhala Dictionary of Buddhism and Zen*, trans., Michael H. Kohn (Boston: Shambhala, 1991), p. 242-43.

12 The term Zen has an interesting history: It is an abbreviation of Zenna, which is a transliterated form of the Chinese *Channa* (or *Chan*); this was, in turn, derived from the Sanskrit *Dhyana,* which means "meditation" and points precisely to the main focus of Zen—meditation on *koans,* mind-bending word games that are meant to provoke deep contemplation on the mysteries of life.

13 Quoted in John C.H. Wu, *The Golden Age of Zen* (Taipei, Taiwan: United Publishing Center, 1975). Also see Philip Kapleau, *The Wheel of Life and Death* (New York: Doubleday, 1989), p. 227.

14 Quoted in Kapleau, Ibid., p. 13.

15 See Manly P. Hall, *Reincarnation: The Cycle of Necessity* (Los Angeles: The Philosophical Research Society, Inc., 1939; reprint, 1986), pp. 46-7.

16 See *Concepts in Transmigration*, ed. Steven J. Kaplan (Lewiston, New York: The Edwin Mellen Press, 1996). See, especially, Chapter Five

(Richard B. Pilgrim, "Mahayana Buddhism," pp.119-132) and Chapter Six (P.D. Premasiri, "The Theravada Buddhist Doctrine of Survival After Death," pp.133-187).

17 Ibid.

18 Ibid.

19 *Lalitavistara,* ed. P.L. Vaidya. Buddhist Sanskrit texts, No. 1 (Darbhanga, Bihar: Mithila Institute, 1958), Chapter XXII, pp. 250, 13-19. Quoted in Martin Willson, *Rebirth and the Western Buddhist* (London: Wisdom Publications, 1987), pp. 13-14.

Chapter 3

Judaism

The souls must re-enter the Absolute,
from whence they have emerged.
But to accomplish this end
they must develop the perfections;
the germ of which is planted in them.
And if they have not developed these traits
in this one life,
then they must commence another, a third,
and so forth.
They must go on like this
until they acquire the condition
that allows them to associate
again with God.
—The Zohar

Not all Jews accept the idea of reincarnation, but the mystical Jewish traditions unabashedly support it. Reincarnation is not directly mentioned in the Hebrew Bible. Belief in an afterlife, however, is evident in many biblical laws. For example, the Bible prohibits necromancy: foretelling the future by communicating with the dead.[1] The existence of such a law and others like it suggests that there was widespread belief in states of existence that were independent of the body, both before and after death. Job 1:20-21 tells us that he came naked from his mother's womb and that he would return to the womb in the same way. Some traditional commentators see this as referring to Mother Earth, meaning that man is made from dust and will return to dust. Other traditionalists, however, see this as a reference to rebirth—a more direct reading of the verse, since the words "mother" and "womb" are used. In Psalms 90:3-6 we find something similar, but without the maternal imagery: "You will turn man back into dust, and will say, 'Return, O children of men.'" In another passage in the Torah (Jeremiah 1:4-5), God tells Jeremiah that he knew him before his birth and that he had consequently allowed him to be born as a prophet.

Such statements are only thin evidence of rebirth in the Bible and are often interpreted by scholars of Jewish thought with no connection to reincarnationist thinking. For this reason, Gershom Scholem, one of this century's best known scholars of Jewish mysticism, states, "There is no definite proof of the existence of the doctrine of *gilgul* ['wheel' of reincarnation] in Judaism during the Second Temple period [in conventional biblical literature]. In the Talmud there is [also] no reference to it."[2]

Jewish scholars acknowledge, however, that certain references are difficult to understand without turning to reincarnation. For example, karmic law and reincarnation seem to be implied by Solomon in Ecclesiasticus 41:9: "Woe be unto you, ungodly men, which have forsaken the law of the most high God! For when you are born, you shall be born to a curse." Solomon also speaks of his own previous merit that resulted in his birth as the son of king: "For I was a wise child, and possessed a good mind. Yea, rather, being good, I came into an undefiled body" (Wisdom 8:19-20). But these verses, too, can be interpreted variously.

Those who are trained in Jewish mystical tradition, or Kabbalah, can find references to rebirth in even the most unexpected holy books. It is said that only those so trained, with intuitive wisdom that comes from decades (if not lifetimes) of serious practice, can penetrate the dense parables and mystical analogies found in biblical literature. Rabbi Gershom Winkler writes that "the 2nd-century mystic Rabbi Shimeon bar Yokhai is reputed to have discovered it [reincarnation] concealed in the following passages from the beginning of chapter 21 in the book of Exodus."[3] One such example: "If a slave is acquired, then for six years shall he serve, and at the onset of the seventh year he should go free without having to pay any ransom. If he came in alone, he shall go out alone. If he was husband to a woman, then shall his wife go out along with him." Rabbi Winkler explains:

> Quoted in the 11th-century classical text on the kabbalah, *The Book of the Zohar*, Rabbi Shimeon demonstrates how these passages "reveal the secrets of reincarnation." The slave represents the reincarnated soul sentenced to come back here and work out some karmic debt. Usually, the repair, the tikkun, is applied to all or any one of the six levels of spiritual gradua-tion (six years), unless the soul is already at the opti-mal seventh level (seventh year), in which instance it is exempt from any karmic debt. And if you did your life independently, the positive and the negative, then as you came in alone, you go out alone. If your rela-tionship with your partner had been such that he or she inspired, empowered—for better or for worse—your personal life choices and actions, then your partner will be allowed to accompany you at no extra cost.[4]

Such interpretive analyses are not uncommon in Jewish history, and where text and tradition are both ambiguous on a given subject, respected rabbis are approached, or even seized upon, for deeper insight.

Flavius Josephus

Although Jewish historians and philosophers have traditionally downplayed immortality and reincarnation, reference to these phenomena can be found throughout Jewish literature. In the first century of the Common Era, for example, the Jewish historian Flavius Josephus wrote about the doctrine of rebirth as if it were a commonly known fact of life:

The bodies of all men are, indeed, mortal, and are created out of corruptible matter; but the soul is ever immortal, and is a portion of the divinity that inhabits our bodies....Do not you know, that those who depart out of this life according to the laws of nature...enjoy eternal fame: that their houses and posterity are sure; that their souls are pure and obedient, and obtain a most holy place in heaven, from whence, in the revolution of ages, they are again sent...into bodies; while the souls of those whose hands have acted madly against themselves are received by the darkest place in Hades?[5]

Josephus writes about the various schools of Jewish thought that existed during his time and how they viewed the nature of the soul. Apparently there was as much diversity of opnion then as now, and this may explain the veiled references found in the biblical literature. The Sadducees, he describes, argued that the soul does exist but that it dies with the body, while the Pharisees believed in the eternality of the soul but that only good men and women were reborn in new bodies— the bad were condemned to eternal punishment. (For the Jews of that period "eternal" was not generally used in a literal sense; it was used figuratively and meant "for a very long time.") The Essenes, claims Josephus, were given to the doctrine of pre-existence and, some say, reincarnation. J.V. Gorres tells us in his *Die Christliche Mystik* that the Essenes were particularly fond of the early *Kabbalah* (or *Cabala*), which is quite clear about its acceptance of reincarnation.[6]

The Kabbalah

The Kabbalah is said to be the mystical, secret wisdom of the Torah and is meant for those Jews who are already accomplished in their spiritual practices. The earliest known Kabbalists flourished in Jerusalem in the third century BC. They belonged to a Jewish sect known as the Tanaiim. Such sects gave birth to some of Judaism's greatest philosophers. Just before the Common Era, in fact, three important Kabbalists appeared on the scene: Jehoshuah ben Pandira;

Hillel, the great Chaldean teacher; and Philo Judaeus, the Alexandrian Platonist. All three openly taught reincarnationist doctrine and are, even today, respected by adherents to all forms of Judaism.

Those in the Jewish tradition who reject the doctrine of reincarnation usually say that while some Jewish mystics apparently support it, the idea was borrowed from non-Jewish philosophies and came to be accepted only in latter-day Judaism. Others ascribe partial credibility: Rabbi Moses Gaster, for example, takes the orthodox position that the teaching of reincarnation does appear to come from early Greek or other classical philosophers, but he adds that it is also an integral part of Jewish thought, possibly originating with Adam himself:

> There cannot be any doubt that these views are extremely old [in Judaism]. Simon Magus raises the claim of former existences, his soul passing through many bodies before it reaches that known as Simon. The Samaritan doctrine of the taheb teaches the same doctrine of a pre-existing soul which was given to Adam, but which, through successive 'incarnations' in Seth, Noah, and Abraham, reached Moses, for whom it was originally formed and for whose sake the world had been created....This doctrine of migration is nowhere to be found systematically developed [in Jewish scriptures]. Wherever it occurs, it is tacitly assumed as well-known, and no explanation is given in detail. It has, therefore, been pieced together and reconstructed by the present writer mostly from the Zoharistic literature....While these are by far the most complete writings, they are by no means the oldest....This brings us to the question of the date and probable origin of this doctrine among the Jews. All the beginnings of esoteric teachings are lost in the midst of antiquity, and, when such doctrines finally see the light of day, they have, as a rule, a long history behind them. It is, therefore, a fallacy to date the origin of metempsychosis among the Jews from the time when it becomes known publicly in the 9th or 10th century. The [Hebrew] masters of the occult science

never doubted its Jewish character or its old origin.
[They asked:] Was it not part of the heavenly mystery
handed down from Adam on through all of the great
men of the past?[7]

There is no doubt, however, that the Kabbalah and its teachings on reincarnation gained wider acceptance in the twelfth or thirteenth centuries, when Jewish mysticism saw a resurgence in many parts of the world (and when, say more conservative scholars, the Kabbalistic literature came into being). Among the many respected Kabbalists who fully support the doctrine of reincarnation and were also influential in mainstream Jewry were Abraham Abulafia (c. 1240-1290); Joseph Karo (1488-1575); Moses Cordovero (1522-1570); Yitzhak Luria (1534-1572); Hayim Vital (1543-1620); Israel Baal-Shem Tov (1700-1760, the founder of the Hasidic movement); Moshe Hayim Luzzatto (1707-1746); and Yahuda Ashlag (1886-1955).

Of all the above, it is arguably Hayim Vital, more formally known as Rabbi Hayim Vittal Calibrese, the 16th-century Italian Kabbalist, who has given the world the most elaborate written documents on reincarnation in the Jewish mystical tradition. More specifically, his work, Sefer (or Sha'ar) HaGilgulim, which literally means, "The Gate of Reincarnation," is clearly one of the greatest Jewish masterworks ever written on the subject. In summary, Calibrese writes that it is only those souls who need to learn very specific lessons that return again and again in multifarious bodies. All souls, says Calibrese, are comprised of six parts, or aspects, which he explains in great detail. Only those parts that require edification come back to the embodied world—the balance of the individual soul's parts rest with the Creator. When all parts of the soul meet their God-given potential, they are liberated, united in the heavenly kingdom. Although this is a simplistic overview of Calibrese's theological view in relation to the soul, it should be noted that he embellished this view with the greatest complexity, so much so that Jewish scholars to this day, even those opposed to reincarnationist doctrine, are hard-pressed to find a more appropriate explanation of Jewish tradition in relation to the nature of the soul and its destination.

Nathan Katz, a noted Jewish theologian, has summarized Calibrese's view: "Birth is possible not only in a human body, but in a stone, a papaya, or a cow—apparently the Judaically-favored embodiments. All gilgulim are educative, not punitive, and one may be liberated from such births through the holy acts of a very pious individual."[8] Katz is somewhat critical, or skeptical, of Calibrese's point of view, but admits its profundity and its constancy in mystical Jewry. Gershon Winkler, cited earlier, is more appreciative of Calibrese's work, noting that his treatise is a veritable "Who's Who of Reincarnation in the Bible"—Calibrese explains who each of the many biblical figures were in previous lives and, often, who they became in their subsequent lives—and a brilliant explanation of the equivalent of feminism in his time as well. Writes Calibrese (as quoted by Winkler):

> Know that the reason the sages of our time are overpowered by their wives is because these holy men are the reincarnated souls of the generation of the Exodus, specifically of those who did not try and stop the dissidents from making the Golden Calf. However, the women of that time declined complicity and refused to surrender their jewelry to the Golden Calf builders. Therefore, these women now reign over their husbands.[9]

Kabbalists of the medieval period recognized three kinds of reincarnation: *gilgul, ibbur,* and *dybbuk. Gilgul* reflects what is commonly understood as reincarnation—a soul enters the fetus during pregnancy. *Ibbur* occurs when a "foreign" soul enters one's body during one's life, staying for some time to accomplish a particular end. When such a soul inhabits a person's body for an evil purpose, the invading soul is called *dybbuk.*[10]

So far as *gilgul* is concerned, the Jewish mystical teachings are similar to those of Hinduism. For example, the *Zohar,* one of the classical Kabbalistic texts, teaches that one's destination at the time of death is largely determined by one's passion throughout life and one's final thoughts just before dying:

> It is the path taken by man in this world that determines the path of the soul on her departure. Thus, if a

man is drawn towards the Holy One, and is filled with longing towards Him in this world, the soul in departing...is carried upward towards the higher realms by the impetus given her each day in this world.[11]

The Kabbalists also believed in a sort of karmic law, although they did not call it that. Rifat Sonsino and Daniel B. Syme, rabbis and scholars both, summarize this in the following way:

The Kabbalists realized that not all righteous individuals in this world receive their due rewards. Some suffer, even though they observe the commandments of the Torah. Reincarnation seemed a plausible answer to this 'injustice.' Some Kabbalists argued that the pain a righteous person suffers in this world is not necessarily a result of personal sins [in this life] but rather a consequence of acts committed in a previous incarnation. This notion was also offered as an explanation for the tragic death of infants....Kabbalists also used reincarnation to explain odd or unusual occurrences of human characteristics. They asked, for example, why some individuals act like animals. The answer offered is that these people carry the soul of a beast....Whereas some Kabbalists believed that reincarnation applied exclusively to human beings, others held that it also included animals and even inanimate objects.[12]

These and related truths can be found throughout the Jewish mystical literature of medieval times. But it was perhaps articulated most eloquently in *The Dybbuk*, a popular play based on Jewish folklore, when one character exclaims, "The souls of the wicked return in the form of beasts, or birds or fish—or plants even—and are powerless to purify themselves by their own efforts. They have to wait for the coming of some righteous sage to purge them of their sins and set them free."[13]

While united in their defense of reincarnation against the more mainstream Jewish philosophers, early Kabbalists were an eclectic lot. Anan ben David, the eighth century founder of Karaism, an important

Jewish sect, spoke blatantly of his reincarnationist beliefs, and although his sect is considered heretical because of its rejection of the Talmud, he was a respected Jewish thinker of his time. Abraham bar Hiyya of Spain, a major Kabbalistic figure from the 12th century, taught that one is reborn, again and again, until one achieves perfection. Many of these early Kabbalists felt that reincarnation was clearly supported by the Hebrew scriptures, which declare that unless one perfectly follows the 613 commandments of the Torah, one cannot secure his place in the world-to-come. This remains even today an important doctrine in mainstream Judaism:

> If a person has not perfected himself by fulfilling all the 613 commandments in action, speech, and thought, he will of necessity be subject to *gilgul* [reincarnation]....Also, whoever has not studied the Torah according to the four levels indicated by *p r d s*, which is a composite of the initial letters from the four words, *peshat,* the literal, *remez,* the allegorical, *derash,* the homiletical, and *sod,* the mystical, will have his soul returned for reincarnation, so that he might fulfill each of them.[14]

Rabbi Menasah ben Israel, although considered something of an eccentric, was greatly respected in his time (the 15th century), and he went even further about the universality of reincarnationist belief:

> The belief in the doctrine of transmigration of souls is a firm and infallible dogma accepted by the whole assemblage of our Church with one accord, so that there is none to be found who would dare deny it....Indeed, there are a great number of sages in Israel who hold firm to this doctrine so that they made it a dogma, a fundamental point of our religion. We are therefore dutybound to obey and accept this dogma with acclamation...as the truth of it has been incontestably demonstrated by the Zohar, and all books of the Kabbalists.[15]

Despite this glittering endorsement, most of the nonmystical Jewish philosophers of medieval times did not seem to want to deal with the subject. Two of the greats, Judah Halevi and Moses Maimonides, virtually ignored reincarnation and its implications. But, again, there were diverse views in the Jewish community of the time. Saadia ben Yosef al-Fayyumi saw the soul and body as an inseparable unit. Abraham ibn Daud expressed a similar idea, adding that bodies that looked alike actually shared one soul. So in medieval Jewry there was clearly a lack of consensus on the nature of the soul and its destination after death.

Concluding Thoughts

In his classic work on rabbinic Judaism, J.F. Moore states: "Any attempt to systematize the Jewish notions of the hereafter imposes upon them an order and consistency which does not exist in them."[16] There were only certain things that were certain: the world in which we live—which is clearly the emphasis of Jewish thought—was known as *haolam hazeh* ("this world"); and the mysteries of afterlife experiences were shoved into the broad category of *haolam haba* ("the world-to-come") or sometimes the even more vague *atid lavo* ("that which is to come"). The larger Jewish communities of non-scholars were left to judge the nature of the soul, pre-existence and rebirth as less important—subjects that could not be penetrated. Jewish philosophy focused instead on morals and ethics, behavior in this world. Jewish philosophers explored the depths of psychology and spirituality, but their focus was clearly this world and how to behave in it. This had certain implications: if it is important to focus on the here-and-now, to be moral and ethical here-and-now, is it not because our behavior has repercussions for the future? Where do we go if we are good? Or if we are bad?

Jewish theology, like its Christian counterpart, has traditionally accepted that in the world-to-come the righteous would be rewarded and the impious would be punished. Jewish tradition teaches that the former would go to paradise (Hebrew: *Gan Eden*), and the latter to hell (Hebrew: *gehinnom*). All Israelites, with very few exceptions, had a place in the world-to-come.[17] There has been some debate about the fate of the non-Jew. Some rabbis have argued that non-Jews have no place in the world-to-come. The prevailing view, however, has been that if a non-Jew is truly righteous, then he, too, has a place in the future life. This latter perspective was accepted by Rabbi Joshua ben Hananiah and even Moses Maimonides and, consequently, largely accepted by the Jewish community. The Talmudic rabbis saw it in the following way: there will be a Day of Judgment for all souls, and on that day there will be, for the pious, a resurrection of the body and soul together. Other rabbis claim that on Judgment Day there will be three groups of living beings. One group is totally righteous (*tzadiqim*), another totally wicked (*rashim*), while the third will be comprised of those with both qualities (*benonim*). The first group will attain everlasting life in heaven; the second is destined for eternal hell; and the third will be born again in a new body (i.e., reincarnate) and gain a chance to perfect themselves. Rabbi Shneur Zalman (the 18th-century founder of Chabad Hasidism) writes in his widely respected work, the *Tanya,* that this third group, the *benoni,* comprise the vast majority of souls in this world. In other words, most people are subject to reincarnation.

But according to the dominant rabbinic view, physical resurrection of the dead will take place "at the end of time" or "when the Messiah comes." The rabbis feel that both body and soul will be brought back to life and jointly subjected to God's final judgment. As Rabbi R. Ishmael writes:

> This may be compared to the case of a king who had an orchard containing excellent early figs, and he placed there two watchmen, one lame and the other blind. He said to them: 'Be careful with these fine early figs.' After some days the lame man said to the blind one: 'I see fine early figs in the orchard.' Said the blind man to him: 'Come let us eat them.' 'Am I then able to walk?' said the lame man. 'Can I then see?' retorted the blind man. The lame man got astride the blind man, and thus they ate the early figs and sat down again each in his place. After some days the king came into that vineyard and said to them: 'Where are the fine early figs?' The blind man replied: 'My lord

the king, can I then see?' The lame man replied: 'My lord the king, can I then walk?' What did the king, who was a man of insight, do with them? He placed the lame man astride the blind man, and they began to move about. Said the king to them: 'Thus have you done, and eaten the early figs.' Even so will the Holy One, blessed be He, in the time to come, say to the soul: 'Why hast thou sinned before Me?' and the soul will answer: 'O Master of the universe, it is not I that sinned, but the body it is that sinned. Why, since leaving it, I am like a clean bird flying through the air. As for me, how have I sinned?' God will also say to the body: 'Why hast thou sinned before Me?' and the body will reply: 'O Master of the universe, not I have sinned; the soul it is that has sinned. Why, since it left me, I am cast about like a stone thrown upon the ground. Have I then sinned before thee?' What will the Holy One, blessed be He, do to them? He will bring the soul and force it into the body, and judge both as one.[18]

It is tales such as this that have created, among many contemporary Jewish thinkers, an acceptance of resurrection as the soul's destiny. As quaint as the story is, it belies a simple notion of the relationship between the soul and the bodily tabernacle in which it dwells. Kabbalists throughout history, in a similar vein, have pointed out that the body is fundamentally unconscious, used by the soul as clothes are used by the body. Consequently, if the soul—the actual living being— comes before God, it will not have to vie with some other entity made of matter in order to win the Lord's consideration. The early Jewish philosopher Philo of Alexandria, mentioned earlier, was particularly outspoken about the soul's immortality and the body's temporality. According to Philo, most souls never come into the world of matter at all, and for the ones that do, their association with the body is a temporary affair, like two strangers fulfilling some vile need.[19] This is clear to Kabbalists and Jewish mystics of various denominations. The Hasidim (or Chassidim), for example, are strong believers in reincarnation and base their belief on works such as the *Sefer Ha-gilgulim* (mentioned earlier) and the *Sefer Ha-Bahir*, Kabbalistic writings that specifically deal with reincarnation and its connection to Jewish thought. Once considered esoteric, these works have entered the common library of Jewish studies, bringing with them answers to age-old biblical riddles about the nature of life and death. Some secrecy prevails, however, as if the more conservative thinkers were trying to keep the doctrine of transmigration an occult oddity and away from the common people. As Gershom Scholem writes:

> The riddle becomes doubly opaque when we recall that the early Kabbalists found in the doctrine of transmigration a solution to the problem of the suffering of the righteous posed by the book of Job. Nahmanides [an important 13th-century rabbi and scholar] wrote an entire commentary to Job, finding the key to the book in this very doctrine, which, according to him, is alluded to in Elihu's discourses to Job. Yet never once does this commentary clearly articulate or even name this doctrine! It does not even use the term *sod ha-ibbur* ('the mystery of passage'), which was generally employed in his circle to describe the theory of transmigration (at least in conjunction with other mysteries). He speaks only of 'a great mystery,' or of 'the level' (*middah*) found here—a rather vague word by which to hint at the matter under discussion. All questions of theodicy, and especially those of the suffering of the righteous and the good fortune of the wicked, are answered by the doctrine of transmigration.[20]

Jewish tradition, then, views reincarnation and indeed all subjects that deal with "the world-to-come" as a mystery, or even an abstraction, to which one is not allowed entrance in this life. However, there is a mystical side to the tradition, known as Kabbalah, which allows its votaries to enter into these mysteries, if somewhat cautiously, and has a great deal to say about the realities of rebirth. Jewish readers are encouraged to study Kabbalistic literature—learning Hebrew if necessary—if they want to know whether or not the Jewish tradition accepts reincarnation as a fact of life.

ENDNOTES

1 See Deuteronomy 18:10-11 and Leviticus 19:31 for examples of such prohibitions.

2 See Gershom Scholem, *Kabbalah* (New York: Quadrangle/New York Times Book Company, 1974), p. 344. Scholem admits, however, that by means of allegorical interpretation, later authorities acknowledged allusions to transmigration in the statements of talmudic rabbis.

3 See Gershom Winkler, "Judaic Perspectives on Reincarnation," in *Concepts of Transmigration*, ed., Steven J. Kaplan (Lewiston, New York: The Edwin Mellen Press,1996), pp. 27-52.

4 Ibid.

5 *The Works of Flavius Josephus,* trans. William Wiston (Philadelphia: J. Grigg, 1835), Vol. II, p. 316 [*The Jewish War*, Book 3, Chapter 8, Number 5.] See also Joseph Head and S.L. Cranston, *Reincarnation: The Phoenix Fire Mystery* (New York: Warner Books, Inc., 1979), pp. 124-5.

6 Regensburg: 1840, III, p. 27.

7 Rabbi Moses Gaster, "Transmigration," in *Encyclopedia of Religion and Ethics*, ed., James Hasting (New York: Scribner and Son's, 1955), Vol. 12, pp. 435-40.

8 See Nathan Katz, Introduction to *Concepts in Transmigration*, op. cit., p. 9.

9 Ibid., Gershon Winkler, p. 35.

10 According to Kabbalistic tradition, *gilgul,* or conventional reincarnation, is common for souls of this world. *Ibbur,* which is less common than *gilgul,* occurs when an invading soul utilizes someone else's body to fulfill a particular religious commandment; *ibbur* is naturally troublesome for the soul whose body is being invaded. Finally, the inauspicious *dybbuk* is a soul whose presence in another's body causes great distress. Kabbalists say that these souls must undergo an exorcism wherein the *baalei shem* ("Master of the Name [of God]") would come in and by chanting the holy name command the evil spirit to leave. See Rifat Sonsino and Daniel B Syme, *What Happens After I Die?: Jewish Views of Life After Death* (New York: UAHC Press, 1990), pp. 46-54. For more on the nature of the *dybbuk,* see Gershom Scholem, *Kabbalah* (New York: Meridian, 1978), p. 349.

11 H. Sperling and H. Simon, trans., *The Zohar II*, 99b (London: Soncino I), p. 324. It is interesting, too, that the soul, in this verse (and generally), is referred to in Hebrew as *neshamah*, which is the feminine form of the noun. Hindu texts also refer to the soul as feminine in relation to God.

12 See Rifat Sonsino and Daniel B. Syme, op. cit., pp. 47-8.

13 See S. Ansky (pseud., Solomon Rapaport, 1863-1920), *The Dybbuk*, trans., G. Alsberg and W. Katzin (New York: Horace Liveright, 1926), p. 81ff. This idea, of course, is also akin to that of the Hindus, who claim that one is free from *karma* by the grace of the *guru,* a powerful sage who teaches one how to engage in spiritual life.

14 (*Shul·an Arukh, Kari'ah beÓokhmat haKabbalah*) Quoted in Ben Zion Bokser, *The Jewish Mystical Tradition* (New York: The Pilgrim Press, 1981), p. 147.

15 Quoted in Joseph Head and S.L. Cranston, op. cit., p. 29.

16 J.F. Moore, *Judaism,* Vol. II (Cambridge, MA.: Harvard University Press, 1962), p. 389.

17 See *Sanhedrin,* 10.1.

18 *Lev., Rabbah* 4.5, Soncino. Quoted in Rifat Sonsino and Daniel B. Syme, op. cit., p. 30.

19 "On the Giants," Philo, *Complete Works*, Vol. II, trans., F.H. Colson and G.H. Whitaker (London: W. Heinemann, 1929), p. 451.

20 Gershom Scholem, *On the Mystical Shape of the Godhead: Basic Concepts in the Kabbalah* (New York: Schocken Books, 1991), p. 208.

Chapter 4

If it can be shown that an incorporeal and reasonable
being has life in itself independently of the body and
that it is worse off in the body than out of it, then
beyond a doubt bodies are only of secondary importance and arise from time to time to meet the varying
conditions of reasonable creatures. Those who require
bodies are clothed with them, and contrawise, when
fallen souls have lifted themselves up to better things
their bodies are once more annihilated. They are thus
ever vanishing and ever reappearing.[1]

—Origen
(Church Father, AD 185-254)

Many modern Christians reject the doctrine of reincarnation
because they feel it is not supported by the Bible. The teaching of
transmigration, they say, is an unnecessary, later addition to biblical
thought, and *Revelation* warns us not to add or subtract anything from
the holy scriptures. It should be noted, however, that this very admo-
nition against tampering with scripture has been the source of much
textual criticism, for modern scholarship has revealed that many books

69

of the Bible were compiled after the *Book of Revelation*.[2] *Revelation* was not always considered the cap on Christianity's canonical literature. And if this is true, then believing Christians may comfortably accept reincarnation, even if it is a later idea.

Let us begin our examination of reincarnation in Christianity with a different premise. Let us suppose that it did not arise after the *Book of Revelation*. There are biblical scholars who claim just that—they say that it preceded *Revelation* and was a part of the "unexpurgated" Bible. Prominent authorities within the Church and scholars from many Christian denominations recognize the possibility that early Christianity may have favored the doctrine of rebirth over that of both resurrection or the existential finality known as heaven and hell.

Leslie Whitehead, an ordained Methodist clergyman and writer, feels that reincarnation in Christianity cannot be proved but that it is not incompatible with the teachings of Jesus.[3] Other contemporary writers who accept reincarnation in the Christian tradition include John J. Hearney, Professor of Theology at Fordham University; William L. de Arteaga, a Christian minister; John H. Hick, Danforth Professor of Philosophy and Religion; Geddes MacGregor, an Anglican priest and Emeritus Distinguished Professor of Philosophy at the University of Southern California; and Quincy Howe, Jr., an Associate Professor of Classics at Scripps College and a graduate of Harvard, Columbia, and Princeton.[4]

Special mention should be made of Edgar Cayce, a well-known Christian writer and once-popular Sunday School teacher, who was given to mystical trances. Many books have been written about Cayce's peculiar psychic abilities, and most researchers have concluded that there is an element of authenticity to them. According to Cayce, Jesus not only believed in reincarnation but reincarnated himself some thirty times before appearing in this world as Jesus of Nazareth.[5] The Association for Research and Enlightenment, founded by Cayce in 1931, has successfully published descriptions and explanations of Cayce's mystic perceptions.

Cayce has provided us with his own vision of reincarnation. Others, more closely aligned with traditional religious views, have also offered their realizations and discoveries. Hans Kung, a prominent, contemporary Catholic thinker, says that Christian theologians "scarcely take this question [of reincarnation] seriously"[6] but asserts that it should be seen as a central issue of Christian theology.[7] While modern Christendom remains divided on this issue, the question we shall address here is not what role does the concept play in contemporary Christian belief, but, rather, is the doctrine of rebirth to be found in early Christian writings, either directly or by implication.

The Bible does not explicitly teach reincarnation. However, many Judaeo-Christian teachings cannot be found in the Bible. For example, the concept of purgatory—which teaches that souls who are not yet perfectly pure may go to "an in-between place" to work out their sins and advance toward heaven—is accepted by all Catholics and many Anglicans, but it is not explicitly mentioned in the Bible. There are no biblical proclamations in direct support of "limbo," either.

The classic example of a widely-embraced Christian concept that has little—if any—biblical basis is that of the Trinity. As Geddes MacGregor, Christian theologian and Emeritus Distinguished Professor of Philosophy at the University of Southern California, points out,

> Except for the text in the first letter of John (1 John 5:7), known to scholars to be a very late interpolation, no direct biblical warrant exists for the doctrine of the Trinity as formulated by the Church. The absence of direct biblical warrant for the doctrine of the Trinity does not mean, however, that the trinitarian formula is antipathetic to the teaching of the New Testament writers. On the contrary, it was held to be, and within Christian orthodoxy it has continued to be accounted, a proper formulation of a great truth about God that is implicit in New Testament teaching. There is no reason at all why the doctrine of reincarnation might not be in a similar case....there is remarkable support for it in scripture, in the Fathers, and in later Christian literature.[8]

Despite Dr. MacGregor's insightful observation, which is supported by other Church scholars and theologians, most pillars of Christian orthodoxy still tend to decry transmigration and discount that it is a truth to be reckoned with. Consequently, history records that only obscure, mystical sects have embraced the doctrine. The Albigenses (Cathari) are the most prominent example. Others include the Paulicians and Bogomils. It was also considered part of the Gnostic creed, based on early apostolic traditions. During the Renaissance, especially, there was a great renewal of reincarnationist thinking among the Christian community; as the Jews were developing their Kabbalistic doctrines, so the Christians were becoming reacquainted with their own mystical traditions. But the Christians were castigated for it by the Church. This reached such severe proportions that Giordano Bruno, one of Italy's leading philosophers and poets of the time, was actually burned at the stake for his belief in reincarnation.

While conventional history relates that it was only small mystic groups and isolated free-thinkers in the Church who supported the teaching of transmigration, there is more to the story than is often told. A picture is now coming into focus in which Christendom embraced reincarnationist teaching from its very inception. This continued to be the case until the Second Council of Constantinople (AD 553), when ecclesiastical authorities had determined that reincarnation was an "inappropriate concept" for the Christian laity. Some details of this council and its subsequent ramifications will be given later in this chapter.

One more important point should be addressed, however, before we explore the details of reincarnation in the Christian tradition, and that point is this: it matters not whether one fits into the Christian mainstream or is considered part of an offshoot sect—one's individual ideas about the hereafter will be determined more by one's thorough knowledge of scripture (or lack thereof) and by one's spiritual insight than by organizational affiliation. Dr. MacGregor elaborates upon this point:

> Those whose thought of God is superficial and whose experience of Him in their lives casual will always have a correspondingly trivial understanding of the nature of the afterlife in which they profess to believe, be it reincarnational or otherwise. Literalistic Christians, whether calling themselves Protestant or Catholic, have conceived of heaven as a place in the sky, inhabited by harp players and paved with golden

streets, with God in the downtown section, replacing City Hall. Such conceptions spring likewise from an impoverished or immature concept of God, to which they are the natural corollary. By the same token, thoughtful Christians need not on their account deny the possibility of an afterlife.[9]

The New Testament

According to the view of most Christian theologians, the prophet Malachi, in the final lines of the Old Testament, predicted what was to happen in the days immediately preceeding the advent of Jesus Christ: "Behold, I will send you Elijah (Elias) the prophet before the coming of the great and dreadful day of the Lord." Malachi wrote these words in the fifth century BC, prophesying the re-appearance of Elijah some four hundred years *after* the time of the historical Elijah. This in itself is indicative of belief in reincarnationist doctrine.

In the first book of the New Testament, Matthew refers to this prophecy on several occasions. In all, the Gospel writers make use of this Elijah prophecy no less than ten times. From these and other New Testament verses it becomes clear that the writers of these books believed that Elijah would indeed "come back" as John the Baptist, and that other ancient Hebrew prophets would ostensibly be reincarnated as well:

> When Jesus came into the coasts of Cesarea Philippi, he asked his disciples, saying, 'Who do men say that I, the Son of Man, am?' And they said, 'Some say that you are John the Baptist; some, Elias; and others, Jeremias, or one of the other prophets.' (Matt. 16:13-14)

> And his disciples asked him, saying, 'Why then say the scribes that Elias must first come?' And Jesus answered them, 'Elias truly shall first come, and he shall restore all things. But I say unto you that Elias has come already, and they knew him not, but have

done unto him whatever they listed. Likewise shall also the Son of Man suffer by their hands.' Then the disciples understood that Jesus was speaking to them of John the Baptist [who had already been beheaded by Herod]. (Matt. 17:9-13)

Verily I [Jesus] say unto you, 'Among those that are born of women there have been none greater than John the Baptist....And if you can understand what I say, he is actually Elias, who was predicted to appear. He who has ears to hear, let him hear.' (Matt. 11:10-11, 14-15)

Despite the nearly blatant references to reincarnationist thinking in these verses, some scholars point to John 1:19-20 in an attempt to override the obvious conclusion. In this scene, John the Baptist is approached by priests from Jerusalem. "And they asked him...'Are you Elias?' And he said, 'I am not.' They then asked him, 'Are you a prophet?' And he answered, 'No.'" Here we find what appears to be John's outright denial of his identification with Elias and even his general prophethood, although the latter has sometimes been interpreted as the Baptist's humility.

When the priests finally gave John the chance to speak for himself, he summarized his reaction to their questions by quoting the prophetic words of Isaiah (40:3): "I am the voice of one crying in the wilderness, 'Make straight the way of the Lord.'" In effect, he does not tell the priests who he really is. Perhaps he was unaware of his previous existence; this is certainly not uncommon. The Baptist's main concern seems to be in trying to give them a deeper answer, one that does not simply involve the parroting of their tradition. He was not *merely* Elias, but Elias with a special mission. Although this interpretation may seem forced, it is the only possible answer. Otherwise it is difficult to reconcile the Baptist's negative reply with Jesus's statement in the book of Matthew, quoted earlier, which clearly identifies Elijah with John the Baptist. Belief in Jesus's words lay at the basis of Christian doctrine, and since he had already confirmed Elijah's identity with John, his conclusion must override the Baptist's own words. Church theologians, in fact, have more or less accepted the above exegesis, for they, too, see the folly in only selectively accepting the words of Jesus.

In another biblical episode, Jesus again seems to endorse reincarnationist thinking. When he and his disciples happened upon a man who was congenitally blind, the disciples inquired from their master, "Was this man born blind because of his sins or because of his parents' sins?" (John 9:2). The very fact that Jesus's primary followers asked such a question presupposes a belief in pre-existence and reincarnation. They accepted, implicitly, that the blind man had existed in another body prior to his birth. Otherwise, how could a man who was born blind have possibly sinned to cause his own condition?

Bible scholar R.C.H. Lenski points out that the reference in this verse definitely points to a specific sin that caused the blindness. The aorist tense of the Greek verb *hemarton,* says Lenski, indicates that someone definitely sinned, whether it be the man who was blind from birth or his parents.[10] Another important biblical scholar, Marcus Dods, explores the implications of this verb *hermarton,* and, as a result, devises five possible explanations: (1) sin had been committed by the blind man in some amorphous pre-existent state; (2) sin had been committed in a previous life, which implies reincarnation; (3) sin had been commited in the womb, after conception but before birth; (4) sin would be committed later in the blind man's life, and the punishment was based on the future act; and (5) the question was one of bewilderment, not to be taken seriously.[11]

Dods is to be commended for considering reincarnation as a possible explanation. John Calvin considered it as a possibility in this verse as well, but ultimately rejected the idea.[12] Scholars Smith and Pink also mention reincarnation as a possible underlying premise behind the question of Jesus's disciples. But a careful study reveals that these writers do not clearly distinguish between reincarnation and other forms of pre-existence, such as life in the womb, so their example cannot be called upon as biblical scholars who support the reincarnationist viewpoint.[13] Geddes MacGregor, however, is quite clear when he writes in relation to this episode that "it must be seen as presupposing a previous life or lives in which the sin had occurred, with these horrible consequences, for there is no other way in which a newborn child could conceivably be supposed to have sinned, unless in the womb, which is absurd."[14]

Despite the certainty of scholars such as MacGregor, there has been a concerted effort among Christian theologians to disparage such inferences to reincarnation. In this case, they point out, Jesus's answer to the disciples revolves around the fact that it was neither the blind man's previous sins nor that of his parents that caused his blindness. Rather, he was born blind so that Jesus could heal him and so that the power of the Lord might thus be glorified.

While it is true that Jesus did answer like this, he in no way indicated that the disciples had asked a foolish or inappropriate question— it would have been the perfect opportunity for Jesus to squelch any allusion to transmigration and other related doctrines. Other passages in the New Testament show that Jesus was not reserved when telling his disciples that their questions were off the mark. If reincarnation were so contrary to biblical teaching, he would have doubtless told them so in relation to this incident. But he did not.

In addition, Jesus's answer may explain why this particular man was born blind, but it does not explain why such a phenomenon occurs in general. Beyond the specific example of the blind man who crossed the path of Jesus and his disciples, others have been born with similar infirmity. Their ailment, no doubt, will not show the glorious works of God in the same way—Jesus may not be there to cure them miraculously. Why are *they* born blind? As cited earlier, Jesus's disciples gave two possible explanations.

There is further allusion to reincarnation in the writings of St. Paul. Commenting on Jacob and Esau, he says that the Lord loved one and hated the other before they were born.[15] It is not possible to love or hate a being prior to his or her coming into existence; if someone does not exist, one cannot love or hate them. It may be argued that anything is possible for God and, defying logic, He could know His feelings toward two beings that have no prior existence. But this answer cannot suffice, for when such a blatant suspension of logical laws occurs in the Bible, the Bible writers attempt to explain the reasons for such suspension. In this instance, however, the verses are left to be taken at face value. And later commentators shed no light on them. Consequently, both Jacob and Esau must have had earthly (or some kind of) existences that predate their known lifetime.

Paul's Epistle to the Galatians can be seen as pointing to reincarnation as well: "Whatsoever a man soweth, that shall he also reap" (6:7). One life is clearly insufficient to reap all that one sows. In addition, it should be remembered that Galatians 6:5 emphasizes the karmic or causal responsibility of our actions. In this same section, right after asserting that one must reap what one sows, St. Paul clarifies further still the way in which such reaping manifests (6:8): "If one sows of the flesh, one reaps of the flesh as well" (i.e., One does not reap results in some incorporeal purgatory, but in another earthly existence.).

While Christian philosophers may have alternative and even reasonable ways to interpret these scriptural quotes, reincarnation is another at least equally sensible explanation with much in its favor. Church doctrine says that heaven, hell, and purgatory are the places where one reaps what one has sown. Is it not possible that rewards and punishments—reactions to our every activity—may be "reaped" in another earthly life? If our "purgatory" is the here and now, then we work out our sins in a succession of lives here on earth.

Likewise, in the *Book of Revelation* 13:10: "He that leadeth into captivity shall go into captivity: he that killeth with the sword must dieth by the sword." Although this is generally taken metaphorically— "if you act sinfully, you will suffer a commensurate reaction"—an alternative and natural extrapolation of this same verse could include the laws of karma (cause and effect) and reincarnation. In fact, if we take this verse literally, as some are inclined to do with other sections of the Bible, then we must accede to the reincarnationist concept. Since many soldiers die peacefully and a long way from the battlefield—nowhere near a sword—retribution must be experienced in a future life for the words of *Revelation* to be true.

Biblical references such as those quoted above prompted Francis Bowen, one of Harvard's most prolific 19th-century American philosophers, to write:

> That the commentators have not been willing to receive, in their obvious and literal meaning, assertions so direct and so frequently repeated as these, but have attempted to explain them away in a non-natural and metaphorical sense, is a fact that proves nothing but the existence of an invincible prejudice against the doctrine of the transmigration of souls.[16]

The Origen Controversy

Many early Church Fathers, such as Clement of Alexandria (AD 150-220), Justin Martyr (AD 100-165), St. Gregory of Nyssa (AD 257-332), Arnobius (*fl.* 290), and St. Jerome (AD 340-420), were advocates of reincarnationist thinking. In his *Confessions,* St. Augustine himself seriously entertained the possibility of reincarnation as an aspect of Christian reality: "Did my infancy succeed another age of mine that dies before it? Was it that which I spent within my mother's womb?....And what before that life again, O God of my joy, was I anywhere or in any body?"[17]

Among the earliest Christian theologians, the most outspoken with regard to reincarnation was Origen (AD 185-254), noted in the *Encyclopedia Britannica*[18] as the most prominent and prolific of all the Church Fathers (with the possible exception of St. Augustine). Christians of great stature, such as St. Jerome, translator of the Latin Vulgate, have glorified Origen as "the greatest teacher of the Church after the Apostles." St. Gregory, Bishop of Nyssa, honored Origen as "The prince of Christian learning in the third century."

What were the views of this influential and consequential Christian thinker in regard to reincarnation? Origen's insights into the subject have been summarized in the now famous Gifford lectures of the Reverend William R. Inge, Dean of St. Paul's Cathedral in London:

> Origen takes the step which to every Greek seemed the logical corollary of belief in immortality—he taught the pre-existence of souls. The soul is immaterial [sic], and therefore has neither beginning of days nor end of life. . . . So convincing is this Platonic faith to him that he cannot restrain his impatience at the crude belief of traditionalists about the last day and resurrection of the dead. How can material bodies be recompounded, Origen asked, every particle of which has passed into many other bodies? To which body do these molecules belong? So, he says scornfully, men fall into the lowest depths of absurdity, and they take refuge in the pious assurance that "everything is possible with God. . . ."[19]

According to the *Catholic Encyclopedia*,[20] Origen's teaching very much paralleled the doctrine of reincarnation as found in the Platonists, the Jewish mystics, and the Hindu religious writings. Religious historian Isaac de Beausobre, in commenting on Origenism, asserts a doctrine that reads almost like a dictionary definition of reincarnation: "It is certain that Origen believed that souls animate several bodies successively, and that these transmigrations are regulated according to the souls' merits or demerits."[21]

Origen himself was quite clear about it:

> By some inclination toward evil, certain spirit souls come into bodies, first of men; then, due to their association with the irrational passions after the alloted span of human life, they are changed into beasts, from which they sink to the level of plants. From this condition they rise again through the same stages and are restored to their heavenly place.[22]

Despite the fact that the early Church Fathers had praised Origen and his teachings—including his view on reincarnation (as cited above)—the Roman Catholic Church came to quite a different view about him soon after his death. It should be pointed out, however, that it was not these sermons on rebirth that initially moved the hands of the powers that be. Rather, it was because Origen had, in a youthful fit of overzealousness, castrated himself for the sake of celibacy. Sainthood, said the ecclesiastical authorities, could never be awarded to one who would harm the body in any way.[23] Origen thus paid a high price for his early fanaticism. But again, it was for this and not his views on reincarnation that the Church refused to canonize him.

But if the price paid by Origen is high, inflation has since engulfed the Church. As a result of his never having officially been declared a saint, Origen's teachings were minimized by those in power. Consequently, his insights on life after death were never accepted by loyal Church followers. Thus the valuable truths taught by an early Church Father were eventually obscured. All of Christendom is still paying for their rejection of Origen.

Such a rejection, however, fit in neatly with the religio-political climate of the sixth century, when Origen's teachings were officially attacked by ecclesiastical authorities. Emperor Justinian (*fl.* AD 527-565), for his own purposes, wanted to rally his subjects around Christianity, the popular creed of his empire. With a preponderance of Origenists, Gnostics, and other reincarnationist sects, however, the emperor felt that Christians might become lax, thinking that they had more than one life with which to attain perfection. If people felt they had the time afforded them by many lives to become serious about their spiritual practices, many would indeed procrastinate adherence to their religion. This would debilitate Justinian's use of Christianity as a political tool.

If they thought they had only one life and after would be subjected to an eternal heaven or hell, Justinian reasoned, then they would again become serious about the goal. And no doubt he could use that earnestness for his own political purposes. Using religion as an opiate with which to unite people was not a new idea, even in Justinian's time. But he went so far as to manipulate certain doctrines and beliefs just to gain secular power. Give them one life only, he said, and then give them heaven or hell.[24] Justinian was sure that this would hasten the Christian resolve to be good "Christians" and thus good citizens, loyal to their emperor.

History cannot sufficiently ascertain whether Justinian's intentions were noble or not, for it is sometimes said that he came to actually believe his own concocted doctrine of "one life and then heaven or hell." Whatever the truth of the situation, his decree against Origen was handed down as a Papal Edict: "If anyone asserts the fabulous pre-existence of souls and the monstrous restoration which follows from it, let him be *anathema* (cursed)."[25] Author and historian Joe Fisher adds his thoughts on this subject with an element of logic:

> Since AD 553, when the "monstrous restoration" of rebirth was denounced by Emperor Justinian, the faithful have been taught to believe in eternal life while ignoring immortality's spiritual sister, reincarnation. Christians learn that eternity starts at birth. But, since only the beginningless can be endless, one might as well have faith in a table's ability to stand on only three legs![26]

Clearly, a table with three legs is a trinity that Christianity can do without.

The Curse Denied

There are those who believe that Origen was never actually condemned by the Church, or that his condemnation was revoked, and that modern Christians may thus adopt his reincarnationist teachings. These views have been elaborately described in *The Catholic Encyclopedia*.[27] Pope Vigilius, the presiding Church authority with Emperor Justinian at the Second Council at Constantinople, is sometimes cited as being nonchalant or even adverse to the decree brought down upon Origenism. In fact, the Pope seemed most reluctant to condemn Origen's teachings and, according to some, eventually revoked his decision against Origenism.

History relates that this particular ecumenical council was convened on May 5, 553, under the presidency of the patriarch of Constantinople with Eastern and Western representatives of the Church to vote on the viability of Origenism (as the doctrine of rebirth came to be called); but Emperor Justinian actually controlled the proceedings. Historical documents reveal that arrangements were made to stack the votes against the Western contingent, most of whom were supporters of Origen's teachings. Of the 165 bishops who signed the decrees against Origenism at the Council's final meeting on June 2, not more than six could have been from the Western side. Pope Vigilius, noting the unfair slant and other irregularities, refused to attend on the day the final decisions were made.

The results have been recorded by theologians and chroniclers of Christian history:

> Opponents of Origenism succeeded in getting the Emperor Justinian to write a letter to the patriarch of Constantinople naming Origen as one of the pernicious heretics. At the command of Justinian, a synod was convened at Constantinople in 543 AD, and an edict was issued, which set forth a list of errors attributed to Origen and purported to refute them. This

edict, which was supposed to promote peace between East and West, divided them further. Pope Vigilius at first opposed the imperial edict and broke off communion with the patriarch of Constantinople who supported it. Then when he arrived in Constantinople he reversed himself and, while being careful not to concede that the emperor had any authority in theological matters, issued a document condemning the writings that had been anathematized in the imperial edict. The document was much criticized by bishops in Gaul, North Africa, and elsewhere, and Vigilius withdrew it in 550 AD [just three years before the council that dealt the final blow to Origenism].[28]

Concluding Thoughts

Since Origen's condemnation was originally revoked by the Pope, there have been Christian historians and theologians throughout the centuries who claim that a believing Christian need not reject Origen and his teachings. In fact, despite official condemnation, Origen's reincarnationist view has been supported by educated Christians both before and after Origen's particular episode. Shelves of books have been written describing the inadequacies of Justinian's perspective, all appealing to scripture and history as well as to logic and common sense. How could a merciful God give His children only one opportunity to reach His kingdom? Would it not be inconsistent with the qualities of an all-merciful God to cast living beings into an eternal heaven or hell, especially after giving us only one chance to redeem ourselves? A loving father will always give his wayward children as many opportunities as possible to come back to him. Is God less of a loving father?

To understand Christian philosophy and how the doctrine of rebirth gradually lost sway in Western religion, let us summarize what we have learned thus far: Western philosophy was originally pro-reincarnationist. The doctrine played a prominent role in the thought of Pythagoras, Socrates and Plato, even if it was eventually de-emphasized and even rejected by Plato's follower, Aristotle—a rejection that served to mold or formulate much of Western thinking. Nonetheless, Plotinus revived reincarnationist ideas with his Neoplatonism, but this only managed to reach esoteric or mystical branches of Western thought (whether Jewish, Christian or Islamic). Because of this and other political reasons (already noted), the rejection of Origenism followed at the Second Council of Constantinople, and the net result was that Aristotelianism was inadvertantly reinforced as the predominant Western world view. This has led to a more or less materialistic conception of the world, where science overshadows religion, and religion focuses more on this world than on the implications of a future (or past) life.

Exactly how this line of thought came into prominence is attributable to the main thinkers of Western (i.e., Christian) philosophy: Augustine, Bonaventure, Duns Scotus, Descartes and John Locke, among others. This unfortunate devolution of Western religion has been documented by many, and it is bound to worsen: there are modern writers, such as Douglas Langston, who foresee, following Gilbert Ryle, that Western thought will eventually deny the soul,[29] for it is reincarnation's logical half-sister. They see this denial as "just a matter of time," and, as a corollary of this denial, that Western religion as we know it may one day come to an end.[30] Consequently, if Christian thinkers do not revert back to Platonic-Augustinian Christianity and the good sense of Origenism, they may one day wake up to find a form of their religion that parallels the materialism they have always countered. Indeed, there may one day be no Christianity that Jesus would even recognize as such.

ENDNOTES

1 For context and elaboration, please see *A Select Library of the Nicene and Post-Nicene Fathers of the Christian Church,* Second Series, VI, Letter CXXIV, Part 15, P. Schaff and H. Wace, eds. (New York: Scribner's, 1900), p. 244.

2 See Pastorals 1 and 2 Peter, James, and others.

3 Leslie D. Whitehead, *The Christian Agnostic* (Nashville: Abingdon Press, 1965), pp. 296-97.

4 See John J. Hearney, *The Sacred and the Psychic: Parapsychology and Christian Theology* (New York: Paulist Press, 1984); William L. de Arteaga, *Past Life Visions: A Christian Exploration* (New York: Seabury Press, 1983); John H. Hick, *Death and Eternal Life* (New York: Harper & Row, 1976); Geddes MacGregor, *Reincarnation in Christianity* (Wheaton, Ill.: Theosophical Publishing House, 1978); and Quincy Howe, Jr., *Reincarnation for the Christian* (Philadelphia: Westminster Press, 1974). All of these writers and a great many more are discussed in Bobby Kent Grayson's unpublished Ph.D. dissertation (Southwestern Baptist Theological Seminary, Fort Worth, Texas, September, 1989), entitled, *Is Reincarnation Compatible with Christianity? A Historical, Biblical, and Theological Evaluation.* While Grayson's work is largely opposed to the idea of reincarnation in the Christian tradition, he does give a fair amount of space to scholars who do not share his opinion.

5 See Jefferey Furst, *Edgar Cayce's Story of Jesus* (New York: Coward-McCann, 1968), p. 71.

6 Hans Kung, *Eternal Life?* (Garden City, New York: Doubleday & Company, 1984), p. 59.

7 Ibid.

8 Geddes MacGregor, *Reincarnation in Christianity*, op. cit., p. 16.

9 Ibid., p. 9.

10 R.C.H. Lenski, *The Interpretation of St. John's Gospel* (Columbus, Ohio: Lutheran Book Concern, 1942), p. 675.

11 Marcus Dods, "The Gospel of St. John," in *The Expositor's Greek Testament* (London: Hodder and Stoughton, 1897; reprint ed., Grand Rapids: William B. Eerdmans Publishing Company, 1980), 1:782.

12 See John Calvin, *The Gospel According to St. John 1-10*, Calvin's Commentaries, trans., T.H.L. Parker (Grand Rapids: William B. Eerdmans Publishing Company, 1961), p. 238.

13 See David Smith, *John, Commentary on the Four Gospels* (Garden City, New York: Doubleday, 1928), p. 165; also see Arthur W. Pink, *Exposition of*

the Gospel of John, Three Volumes (Swengel, PA., I.C. Herendeen, 1945; reprint ed., Grand Rapids: Zondervan Publishing Company, 1968), 2:64-65.

14 See Geddes MacGregor, *Reincarnation as a Christian Hope*, Library of Philosophy and Religion (London: Macmillan & Company, 1982) p. 43.

15 See Romans 9:10-13; Malachi 1:2-3.

16 Francis Bowen, "Christian Metempsychosis," *Princeton Review*, May 1881.

17 *The Confessions of St. Augustine*, Book I, Edward B. Pusey, trans., *Harvard Classics* (New York: P.F. Collier, 1909), p. 9.

18 *Encyclopedia Britannica*, 11th Edition, German theologian Adolf Harnack's article on Origen.

19 W.R. Inge, *The Philosophy of Plotinus* (London: Longmans Green, 1948), II, pp. 17-19.

20 *Catholic Encyclopedia*, 1913 Edition, IV, pp. 308-9. See also XI, p. 311.

21 Isaac de Beausobre, *Histoire Critique de Manichee et du Manicheisme* (Amsterdam: 1734-1739), II, p. 492.

22 Origen, trans. B.W. Butterworth, *On First Principles*, Book I, Chapter VIII (New York: Harper & Row, 1966), p. 73.

23 See Martin Larson, *The Story of Christian Origins* (Washington, DC: Joseph J. Binns/New Republic, 1977).

24 Ibid.

25 The anathemas have been reprinted in their entirety in *A Select Library of the Nicene and Post-Nicene Fathers*, op. cit., XIV, pp. 318-20, and also in eds., Joseph Head and S.L. Cranston, op. cit., pp. 321-5.

26 Joe Fisher, *The Case for Reincarnation*, Preface by the Dalai Lama (New York: Bantam Books, 1985), p. 2.

27 *Catholic Encyclopedia*, op cit., XI, p. 311.

28 Geddes MacGreggor, op. cit., p. 56.

29 See Dougles Langston, "The Western Philosophical Tradition," in Concepts of Transmigration, op. cit., pp. 13-25.

30 Ibid.

Chapter 5

I slam

I died as mineral and became a plant,
I died as a plant and rose to animal,
I died as animal and I was Man.
Why should I fear? When was I less by dying?

—Jalalu' l-din Rumi
(1207-1273)

The Qur'an does not offer a consistent doctrine of death or rebirth, and this has led some scholars, even among the orthodox, to question whether the Prophet Mohammed had any comprehensive knowledge of these subjects.[1] The larger theological and philosophical issues dealing with the nature of existence and life after death are only briefly dealt with in the Qur'an, but later theologians and commentators had much to say, systematizing the implicit meaning in the traditional stories of the Prophet (*Hadith*) as well as Qur'anic truths. In this way, the Islamic tradition followed the route of its parent faiths, Judaism and Christianity, which also depend quite a bit on later commentaries. Islam reveres both the Old and New Testaments; so, many of the arguments given for reincarnation in these scriptures might also apply to Islam.

87

Adherents of mainstream Islam, like those of Judaism and Christianity, cling tenaciously to prevailing conceptions of death and the afterlife, and few are willing to peruse the mystical literature to find the underlying or inner meaning of Qur'anic teachings in this regard. And so, as in Judaism and Christianity, it stands:

> An elaborate system of Muslim beliefs about the nature of death, the process of dying, and the events of the grave immediately following death developed in the early centuries following the death of Mohammed [seventh century C.E.]. Orthodox Muslims reached general agreement regarding the order of events, the identity and roles of the various celestial and infernal beings who greet the deceased, extract his soul, interrogate him about his faith and works, and even create a state of bliss or punishment within the grave.[2]

As in most religions, Islam teaches that God does not just create man so that he can one day die—there is a conception of rebirth and renewal found throughout the Qur'an and the Islamic tradition. A well-known verse from scripture says: "He is the one who gave you life (*ahyakum*), then He will cause you to die (*yumitukum*), then He will give you life (*yuhyakum*) [again]." This same idea occurs later in the Qur'an as a warning for idol worshippers: "It is God who created you (*khalaqakum*), then provided for you, then He will cause you to die (*yumitukum*), then He will give you life (*yuhyikum*) [again]. Can any of the images [you claim to be God] do any of these things? Glory be to Him!" While these scriptural references and others like them appear clear in their support of reincarnation, they are traditionally interpreted as allusions to resurrection.

The Problem of Resurrection

In the Qur'an, references to resurrection abound, but one wonders if these verses could have at one time referred to reincarnation. For example, in Sura 20:55/57, God speaks to Moses: "Out of the earth have We created you, and We will return you into it and then bring you forth (*nukhrijukum*) from it a second time." This verse is traditionally seen as pointing to the theory of resurrection but may as readily be interpreted to mean that the body is repeatedly created and destroyed and that the soul after death will again be born in physical form. Islamic tradition views the living being as a soul (*nafs*) that is animated by a spirit (*ruh*). The ambiguity is further complicated by the many definitions of the word *nafs*: the soul, the self, the blood, the living body.[3] While the theological borders between body, soul and intellect are somewhat vague in Islamic belief, the immortal soul has always been central to traditional Qur'anic thought. Sufis and other Islamic mystics have interpreted the texts from a reincarnationist point of view, and we will return to the mystics and their perspectives after more thoroughly looking at mainstream Islamic views on death and the life hereafter.

According to the Qur'an as it is traditionally interpreted, wayward souls are questioned by angelic messengers of Allah (God) immediately after death. Regardless of the relative good qualities found in "the faithless," disbelief in Allah and His prophet causes them to be cursed and sentenced to eternity in Jahannam, the Islamic counterpart to the Jewish and Christian Gehenna, or hell. Like their Judaeo-Christian forebears, the Muslim faithful see Jahannam as an afterlife condition of fiery torment. While the punishment does not fully manifest until after the "final resurrection," the Qur'an explains in no uncertain terms that unbelievers, immediately after death, get a taste of the eternal hell that awaits them.

The souls of those who believe in Allah and His prophet do not receive the same kind of interrogation from the angels of death. The angels come before the righteous and welcome them to heaven. "Enter the Garden [*al-janna*]," they say, "for all the good that you have been doing."[4] Once again, the heavenly rewards for pious Muslims will not be fully realized until after the final resurrection, but unlike the nonbelievers, the righteous are said to rest peacefully until the allotted hour.

As the Islamic tradition developed, theologians interpreted the rewards and punishments that came immediately after death as a sort of condition of the soul in the grave while it awaited resurrection. After burial, the tradition teaches, two angels named Munkar and Nakir, who have black faces, voices like thunder, piercing blue eyes, and long hair that extends to the ground, come and visit the living being in the grave and ask about the pious or impious acts he or she performed during life. This is called "the trial of the grave" and is anticipated by all believing Muslims.

To prepare for this trial, concerned relatives and friends—funeral mourners—whisper advice into the ears of the deceased in order to elicit the appropriate answers for the departed's heavenly interlocutors. If the deceased deals with the trial successfully, he or she will experience "the heavenly garden" while still in the grave; if not, he or she will endure untold torment while in the grave. In due course, however, both will undergo a "new creation" in preparation for the resurrection, at which time the righteous and the nonbelievers go to their respective places in heaven or hell. This is the mainstream view on death and afterlife in contemporary Islam, and it has been so for several centuries.

Death or Divine Sleep?

In the early days of Islam, Muslim theologians had a much simpler conception of death, comparing it to sleep. While notions of resurrection played a part in this earlier view of the afterlife, they were less clearly defined than later conceptions and lend themselves without strain to reincarnationist interpretation. The only idea that was consistently maintained by early Muslim theologians was this comparison of death and sleep:

> The problem of determining the Qur'anic view of the nature of death is closely related to two other questions: the relationship between death and sleep, and the existence of the soul. Faced with the timeless mysteries of life and death, the Qur'an adopts the ancient notion of likening death to sleep and waking to resurrection from the dead, as in 25:47/49: "It is He who has made the night to be a mantle for you, and sleep for a resting, and has made the day for a rising (*nushur*)." The night is a garment that covers a person while he is sleeping; sleep is a sign of death, and dawn (when the person awakens) is a sign of resurrection (*nushur*)...[5]

The pivotal term here is *nushur*, which actually means "rising" or "rousing." The term came to be associated with resurrection by latter-day Islamic philosophers who were trying to reconcile prevailing theories of heaven and hell with traditional Qur'anic exegesis. However one interprets words such as *nushur*, the early Islamic view of death as sleep is unabashedly reincarnationist: one who sleeps will eventually wake up! Whether one wakes up in a sort of ultimate resurrection or in a cycle of births and deaths is fodder for theological debate; but the post-death experience was prominent in early Islamic thought. Today's mainstream Muslims lean toward the resurrectionist interpretation. Islamic mystics such as the Sufis, on the other hand, have always understood the post-death experience as reincarnation, and *nushur* as the soul repeatedly rising again in new bodies.

In Islam, reincarnation is referred to as *tanasukh,* but it is rarely mentioned by conventional Muslim philosophers. Arab and Persian theologians, much like their Jewish Kabbalistic counterparts, opined that transmigration was a plausible consequence of an evil or unfulfilled life.[6] The idea of *tanasukh* is more widespread among Muslims in India, obviously because of the Hindu influence, but it is seen in the writings of seers and mystics from Arabia and other parts of the world as well. Even the Qur'an, say Islamic supporters of transmigration, is supportive of reincarnationist doctrine, as we see in these examples:

> We said to him who broke the Sabbath, 'Be you an ape, despised and hated' (2:65). Worse is he whom Allah has cursed and brought His wrath upon, and whom He has turned into apes and swine (5:60). Allah has caused you to grow as a growth from earth, and afterwards he makes you return thereto, and he will bring you forth again (71:17-18).[7]

The inner meaning of these and other verses has been analyzed by prominent Persian Sufi poets such as Jalaluddin Rumi, Saadi and Hafiz.[8] Mansur al-Hallaj of the 10th century, considered one of the pre-eminent Sufi thinkers of all time, is remembered for his deeply spiritual poetry in which reincarnation was often a theme:

Like the herbage I have sprung up
many a time on the banks of flowing rivers.
For a hundred thousand years I have lived
and worked and tried in every sort of body.

The Druze

The Druze, who were known as the Sufis of Syria, accepted reincarnation as a fundamental principle underlying much of their theology. This syncretic and heretical offshoot of Islam, founded in the 11th
century by the Fatimid caliph al-Hakim, is mostly practiced by people
living in Lebanon, Jordan and Syria, but it is having a more and more
marked influence on traditional Muslims who come into contact with
it because of its deep sense of spirituality and its connection to ancient
doctrines that were considered lost to modern adherents.

It should be remembered that the persecution of non-Christian
scholars by the medieval Church had gradually driven most students
of science and philosophy out of Europe. Some migrated to Persia,
others to Arabia, and still others to India. The Christian Gnostics influenced the Arabs with Greek philosophy and its derivative Gnosticism;
the Nestorians introduced the Neoplatonic philosophies to the Arabs;
and the exiled Jews brought them the Kabbalistic literature. The teachings of Hermes, too, infiltrated the Middle East during this same
period, while Alberuni went to India and learned the religious classics
of that land, many of which were then translated into Arabic and
Persian languages and made their way back to Arabia. So by the time
of the Druze "heresy," the doctrine of rebirth had already come and
gone, and it was difficult to discern what was heresy and what were
the original teachings of the Qur'an.

The faithful started to look for internal and esoteric meanings of
scripture. Mohammed himself affirmed that the Qur'an had an
esoteric foundation: it was "sent in seven dialects; and in every one of
its sentences there is an external and an internal meaning....I received
from the messenger of God two kinds of knowledge: One of these I
taught...[but] if I had taught them the other it would have broken their
throats."[9] The inner meaning of many texts included a reincarnation
sensibility, but this was lost over the course of time.

Reincarnation As Heresy

In a series of articles, "Reincarnation—Islamic Conceptions," M.H. Abdi, a Muslim scholar, points to the specific events that led to the expulsion of reincarnation as a doctrine in mainstream Islam:

> The position adopted by the successive luminaries who followed [Mohammed] was to affirm the belief in reincarnation but not to propagate it as a teaching for the masses. This attitude was due to psychological reasons. The emphasis in Islamic teachings has throughout been on the purity of action....Another factor to remember is that the defensive wars, which have been described as Jehad or holy wars, which the Muslims fought in the early days and the wars of conquests (therefore not holy) which the Muslims fought in later days . . . gave a different shift to Islamic teachings. Philosophical, mystical, and ethical teachings received an impetus in the first phase but they had subdued existence in the later phase. During this phase the republican character of the State was changed into monarchy and the supremacy no more belonged to the saints and philosophers. A subject like reincarnation demands a subtle mental attitude. It entails understanding of the higher planes of consciousness, the laws of cause and effect, and the working of the laws of evolution. The monarchs had no interest in such subjects. Like so many other teachings, reincarnation was confined to the study and attention of the outer and inner students of Sufism...[However,] there is no danger for a Muslim being called a heretic if he believes and expresses himself in favour of reincarnation.[10]

Adherents of traditional Islamic sects did indeed fear the heretic label, and so reincarnation, to this day, is generally discussed only in the Sufi tradition, as mentioned earlier. Among the traditional theologians, however, many found it difficult to reconcile Islamic morals and religion without including a doctrine of reincarnation. G.F. Moore, for example, states in his Ingersoll lecture on transmigration that "among Mohammedans the difficulty of reconciling the sufferings of innocent children...with the goodness or even the justice of God led some of the liberal theologians (Mu'tazilites) to seek a solution in sins committed in a former existence....Reincarnation is fundamental to the doctrine of Imam[11] as held by the [Shi'ites]; it was developed in a characteristic form by the Ism'ilis, and is a cardinal doctrine of Babism."[12]

Islamic historian E.G. Browne elaborates these ideas in his classic three-volume work, *The Literary History of Persia*. While discussing the more esoteric schools of Islam, he outlines three forms of transmigration accepted by classical Muslim thinkers: (1) *Hulul*, the periodical incarnation of a saint or prophet; (2) *Rij'at*, the immediate return of an Imam or any other important spiritual leader after death; and (3) *Tanasukh*, the ordinary reincarnation of all souls. The Ismailis even claim that the Hindu God Krishna incarnated as the Buddha and then as Mohammed, while others within this same sect believe that great teachers repeatedly incarnate for the benefit of successive generations. This doctrine is articulated in various ways by a majority of Muslim religious leaders. When pressed, many contemporary Muslim religionists condone, at least in theory, belief in the other forms of reincarnation outlined by the mystics. Like other Western traditions, Islam relegates reincarnation to the background, often considering belief in it to be at worst heretical and at best a subject for mystics and other eccentrics; however, a careful study of Islam's various traditions and theological writings reveals that reincarnation is an integral part of its fundamental message to the world.

Concluding Thoughts

We conclude with the insightful and hopeful words of Muslim theologian Earl Waugh:

> Reincarnational notions reside in the rich texture of Islamic culture and are the product of its sophistication; they are not an 'add on.' At the same time, even

those who diverged far enough from the borderlines of orthodoxy to be designated as different religions [i.e., Sufism] were not outside the pale primarily because of a strict reincarnational viewpoint; rather, they were responding to a number of influences that, in some ways, were generated out of pressures within Muslim history and culture. We can see this most evidently in the search for a leadership that has the stamp of divinity or divine knowledge within it. Based on this analysis, it would seem safe to predict that these persistent fragments will not only continue, but will take on fascinating new forms as they respond to other contexts, both nurtured within Islam and in reaction to its pressures.[13]

ENDNOTES

1 See Hartwig Hirschfield, *New Researches into the Composition and Exegesis of the Quran* (London: Royal Asiatic Society, 1902), pp. 41-2.

2 Alford T. Welch, "Death and Dying in the Qur'an," in *Religious Encounters with Death*, eds., Frank E. Reynolds and Earle H. Waugh (University Park and London: The Pennsyvania State University Press, 1977), p. 183.

3 See David Chidester, *Patterns of Transcendence: Religion, Death, and Dying* (Belmont, California: Wadsworth Publishing, 1990), p. 207.

4 Ibid., p. 208. Also see Qur'an, Surah 16:28-32.

5 Alford T. Welch, *op. cit.*, p. 187.

6 Benjamin Walker, *Masks of the Soul* (Wellingborough, Northamptonshire: The Aquarian Press, 1981), p. 37.

7 For more such Qur'anic references, see Ibid., p. 38-9.

8 Ibid., p. 38.

9 "Broken their throats" was a popular saying of the period, meaning that it would "put them in utter confusion." See *The Hadith of Mohammed* as quoted in Nadarbeg K. Mirza, *Reincarnation and Islam* (Madras: 1927), pp. 4-5.

10 *Theosophy in Pakistan* (Karachi: October/December, 1965).

11 The Imam is one of a succession of religious leaders believed by the Shi'ites to be divinely inspired. "The Imam is supposed to be a reincarnation of a divinity formerly manifest in Mohamet," according to the *New Oxford Dictionary*, "Reincarnation" (eds.). Quoted in Joseph Head and S.L. Cranston, *Reincarnation: The Phoenix Fire Mystery* (New York: Warner Books, 1979), p. 167.

12 See G.F. Moore, *Metempsychosis* (Cambridge: Harvard University Press, 1914), pp. 52-4.

13 Earl Waugh, "Persistent Fragments: The Trajectories of Reincarnation in Islam," in *Concepts of Transmigration*, op. cit., pp. 53-85.

Afterword

The preceding chapters have attempted to show that the major world religions have at one time or another all accepted the doctrine of reincarnation, and that political circumstances, scriptural interpolation, or even brute sectraian pride have periodically relegated these teachings to a sort of peculiarity associated with mysticism, or at least forced it to be seen as a dated concept, lost in historical oblivion. The Eastern religions and the esoteric or mystical traditions of the West have, for the most part, fared better than the rest in maintaining a sensibility of transmigration. However, this is not because of some strange fetish or peculiarity but rather because these schools of thought tend to place an emphasis on philosophy as a necessary adjunct to ritual.

Modern mainstream Western religions, reflecting the culture in which they thrive, offer a very linear conception of reality: we have a beginning and an end, and everything submits to this rigid structure. The choices are few: birth to death, to heaven or hell, and that's it. Such a definition of time includes only a beginning and an end. Questions of what comes after have no real standing. Aristotelian thought is the rule of the West.

Nature shows us, however, that linear conceptions of reality are inadequate. The cycles of the sun around the horizon during the course of the year suggest a different notion of time—one that is ongoing, without beginning or end.[1] The hands on a watch do not stop after a full day has passed, they go on and on; the days of the week issue forth again and again; the seasons recur; the *yugas,* or huge periods of cosmic time, duplicate themselves; all experiential knowledge suggests a cyclic truth to reality.

Cyclical time applies to the microcosm as well as to the macrocosm. Each living being plays his round in life—and then goes where? Does he or she defy nature and simply cease to exist? Does a person accept some strange linear fate which has nothing to do with observable reality? Or does the wandering soul go for another round in the cycle of *samsara,* like the ever-changing seasons? Do people reincarnate, like all other facets of existence, or are living souls some weird, aberrant phenomenon that end with the body?

As more scientists explore the ramifications of cyclical reality, they tend to concur with the Eastern and mystical traditions of the world, which assert that the soul transmigrates from one body to another. Writes Gary Zukav in *The Dancing Wu Li Masters:*

> Every subatomic interaction consists of the annihilation of the original particles and the creation of new subatomic particles. The subatomic world is a continual dance of creation and annihilation, of mass changing to energy and energy changing to mass. Transient forms sparkle in and out of existence, creating a never-ending, forever-newly-created reality.[2]

Research analyst Joe Fisher interprets the above in the following way:

> Science advances the hypothesis that a microscopic form of rebirth underlies everything in the physical world. In *The Tao of Physics*, Fritjof Capra refers to these subatomic particles as being 'destructible and indestructible at the same time.' This is precisely what is implied by reincarnation: even as we die we are capable of activating another body. Destructible yet indestructible. Dead yet very much alive.[3]

In recent years, hypnotic regression and other realms of psychical research have shed much light on reincarnationist phenomena. There has been a good deal of fraud in this area, but great strides have been made toward proving reincarnationist doctrine, especially when no other reasonable explanation exists for a particular testimony of past-life regression. The amount of such material is enormous. Young children know geographical locations, languages and people that they could not have possibly known from this one lifetime. Trained experts check their stories and, to their amazement, cannot disprove their veracity. Sometimes, though rarely, a person under hypnosis will be brought back to youth, childhood, and beyond, giving details of language and location unknown in the subject's waking state.

Dr. Ian Stevenson

There have been many researchers, psychiatrists and hypnotherapists who began with little or no sympathy for reincarnationist perspectives, but their research unavoidably pointed in this direction, and so, like it or not, they proceeded with their findings. The work of Dr. Ian Stevenson is particularly representative of this approach. Stevenson, who was chairman of the Department of Neurology and Psychiatry in the School of Medicine at the University of Virginia, later became Carlson Professor of Psychiatry in their Department of Behavioral Medicine and Psychiatry, where he eventually went on to be Director of the Division of Personality Studies. His research of childhood reincarnation cases—his specialty, since children are generally more apt to have less "blockage" and thus respond better than adults to past life regression techniques—spans some 30 years and several continents. Although many of the children he has worked with are from India and Sri Lanka, others are from the Middle East, Europe, Africa and the Americas. As of 1987, Stevenson had accumulated over 3,000 cases of this type in his files, and slightly over half of these are of the "solved" type (i.e., the child's past life experience had been determined beyond reasonable doubt). In the 64 such solved cases from India, Sri Lanka, Lebanon, Turkey, Thailand and Burma—about which he has written extensively—the children's parents or relatives were typically able to recall up to 60 statements made by the child that were mostly capable of verification and which helped identify his or her past life.

While Stevenson was initially something of a skeptic, he has uncovered hundreds of cases of this type, cases that can only be explained in terms of reincarnation. And so, with the passion of a religious mystic, he pursues the research of his chosen field, even though he risks being branded a heretic and being ostracized from the fellowship of his more mainstream colleagues—indeed, he has been seriously ridiculed by his colleagues, as we shall soon see. (As a side note, if this sounds like the same problem that is faced by religious mystics in the West, it is. But Stevenson cannot be accused of being a crank, a religious fanatic, or a young whipper-snapper involved in some contemporary fetish! He is a respected scientist, without religious bias, and in his seventies. His research is objective, and those who wish to inform themselves of his scientific approach to reincarnation should read his many published reports and books on the subject.)

His work first caught the public eye in 1960, when he published a 44-page essay, "The Evidence for Survival from Claimed Memories of Former Incarnations," which won a much-honored prize from the American Society for Psychical Research. Throughout the 60s and 70s, Stevenson continued to conduct extensive research, which came to be respected by colleagues, both those predisposed to reincarnation and those who began as determined skeptics. Thanks to Stevenson's work, thousands of cases "suggestive of reincarnation" have now seen their way into print, and his related work is published in such prestigious academic journals as *The Journal of Nervous and Mental Disease, The Journal of the American Medical Association,* and *The International Journal of Comparative Sociology.*

Stevenson now joins hundreds of scientists and millions of laymen who believe that "reincarnation could account for certain behavior not explained by genetics and early environmental influences."[4] Dr. Harold Lief, one of Stevenson's colleagues, describes him as meticulous, thorough, methodical, and objective. If anyone can discover the truth of reincarnation without bias, says Lief, it will be Stevenson. Notwithstanding the attempts of several well-known scholars—such as John Hick and Paul Edwards—to dismiss a part of Stevenson's work, particularly that involving children, Stevenson's results are thus far quite impressive. The part of Stevenson's work to which the above critics object centers around certain young subjects, usually around six years of age, who sometimes, under hypnosis or, in rare cases, spontaneously, speak as if they were someone else who had died a few years previously. Critics point to the overactive imaginations of children, who like to "pretend to be" someone else, or they refer to the possible harmful effects such experiments might have on those so tender in years. Also, it seems likely, they say, that young children can be easily influenced to believe anything, and, it is well-known, that children are highly impressionable as well.

Even the few remaining Stevenson critics, however, cannot explain how these children, who are often so young that they are just learning their native tongue, can, in these rare cases, speak fluently a language with which they are otherwise unfamiliar. Moreover, these "cases of the reincarnation type" are not isolated incidents but were studied in depth by Stevenson from the 1960s into the 1990s—varied cases for over thirty years. He and his colleagues have found that in about half of over 3,000 cases in his files, the "other people" that these children "pretend to be" are often historically specific people who had died before the children were born.

And it's not as if Stevenson is alone. At the time of his research, the field of hypno-regression therapy was gaining in popularity among psychologists and psychiatrists as a tool for curing or alleviating troubling conditions such as phobias, compulsions, obesity, nightmares and medically unexplained pain. Upon hypno-regression, the causes of the ailments were sometimes found to be rooted further in the past than in the patient's childhood. Only by going ever further back—into one or more of the patients' past lives—would the cause of the patient's symptoms be uncovered and brought into the open for both patient and doctor to perceive. In short, it required hypno-regression for the patient's ailment, which usually had persisted even if a good deal of conventional therapy had been applied, to disappear. As the psychotherapists involved in such studies gained experience from the hundreds of patients and thousands of past lives recorded in their files, they realized how astounding and important the phenomenon actually is. By the early 1990s, dozens of authoritative books on the subject had appeared for public consumption.

Around this time, too, the phenomenon of near-death experiences (NDEs) had started to become widely known. This refers to the subjective experience of people who have had a close brush with death, validating for them the existence of an inner self, a higher self, or a soul—the "real you"—which can survive outside the body and retain all memories related to the body. These NDEs tended to overlap with the findings of those hypno-therapists who regressed their patients back to the time of death within a past life, and then went forward from there towards the stage in-between life and death. The amazing thing here, despite a good deal of forgery, is the fact that many people experiencing NDEs had similar stories to tell, almost identical descriptive accounts of perception in the in-between state. And these people were separated by time, country, language, and economic status—so it is highly unlikely that they conspired to tell some untruth for reasons that skeptics might consider plausible.

From the scientific perspective, any non-understood phenomenon that seems unexplainable—even if it is vouched for by lay witnesses—is likely to be attacked by members or sympathizers of the Committee for the Scientific Investigation of Claims of the Paranormal (CSICOP). Reincarnation is such a phenomenon, as it involves a transfer of detailed memories from one life to a later life through some means (by the "spirit," "psyche," or "soul") that has been up to this point inaccessible to physical measurement. Thus, Stevenson himself—and many others who do similar work—has come under verbal and literary attack by supporters of this organization. His studies have been denigrated more than anyone else in this field because he has done much more than any other to bring these child-hood cases to popular attention.

According to Arthur Berger, director of the International Institute for the Study of Death, in an essay in CSICOP's journal, the *Skeptical Enquirer*, one never really knows if "any particular investigator is sane, honest, objective, or competent, or whether he is fraudulent or has been deceived."[5] Although this peculiar fact needs to be kept in mind for those whose backgrounds, research techniques and/or find-ings are obscure or unverifiable, there was no cause for him to have applied it to Stevenson, whom he had to concede had never been accused of wrongdoing. This is an example of the messenger being attacked when the message is found unacceptable to a person's belief system.

One thing Berger failed to mention with relation to Stevenson is that he (Stevenson) had many first-hand (and first-rate!) collaborators over the years. These fellow researchers would also have to be accused of improper investigations—if he were to so accuse Stevenson—but there has been no basis for doing so. Moreover, there have been ample numbers of qualified U.S. professionals within Stevenson's field who have reviewed his findings and found them to be quite carefully researched, containing evidence that should not be ignored.

It should be reiterated that cases of the reincarnation type have been investigated first hand by others, independently of Stevenson. Recent cases have been investigated by Dr. Erlunder Haraldsson of the Department of Psychology, University of Iceland, Reykjavik. He looked into 20 cases in Sri Lanka; nine of these were solved, four of them by Haraldsson himself, with the aid of four different interpreters. He noted many similarities of these cases, involving mostly Buddhists, with the many cases reported by Stevenson.

Another investigator is Dr. Antonia Mills, Department of Behavioral Medicine and Psychiatry, University of Virginia at Charlottesville. In one study of ten children in northern India, she found all ten cases to be solved, with conclusive evidence that none of these cases were the result of fraud or fantasy, or of projection of an alternate personality in response to any persuasions from the family. In a further study of 26 cases involving a Muslim background of the subjects in northern India, Mills found 17 to be solved. Of these, four were children raised in Muslim families but whose past life had been Hindu, six were children raised in Hindu families but whose past life had been Muslim, and in seven cases both the children and their past lives were Muslim.

Yet another investigator, Dr. Jurgen Keil of the Psychology Department of the University of Tasmania, Australia, investigated 23 new cases from Burma, Thailand and Turkey, using interpreters during interviews. Of these, 12 can be classed as "solved." Keil noted that his own belief system is one which accepts the finality of death, so he preferred to speak of "paranormality" being involved rather than the possibility of reincarnation. Thus, he concluded that some children and their families report "information that links the children to other persons who had previously died, and that some of this information could only have been gained by what one would call paranormal means." He also concluded that "It is now sufficiently clear that the positive results obtained by IS [Ian Stevenson] cannot be readily dismissed by suggesting that IS may have intentionally or unintentionally misrepresented some aspects of his research."6

Thus, Berger's attempt to attribute the data of Stevenson's cases to one man, whose competence might then be questioned, was clearly misguided and perhaps motivated by Berger's own preconceived notions. Berger further failed to note the corroborative evidence in regard to Stevenson's work, much of which is as impressive as Stevenson's work itself. All of this information is nicely summarized in the work of James W. Deardorff, in his book, *Jesus in India: A Reexamination of Jesus' Asian Traditions in the Light of Evidence Supporting Reincarnation* (San Francisco: International Scholars Publications, 1994).

The Bloxham Tapes

Evidence for reincarnation that parallels that of Ian Stevenson's work is to be found in the now famous Bloxham tapes—the regressions recorded by Amall Bloxham, a respected hypno-therapist of Cardiff, Wales, who believes that scores of his subjects under hypnosis remembered and re-lived their previous lives. The difference between Bloxham and Stevenson is that Bloxham had always believed in reincarnation, but his subsequent findings are nonetheless objective and worthy of consideration. A television producer, Jeffrey Iverson, has written a book about the Bloxham experiments, and a documentary film has been made of the taped material as well. For a brief period, the Bloxham tapes were seriously considered by a small but highly regarded group of researchers; but when the tapes became the rage of popular tabloids, they were dismissed as more faddish than anything else, and the actual content, which speaks volumes, came to be ignored. The work of Bloxham was nicely summarized by Benjamin Walker (*Masks of the Soul,* op. cit.), and what follows is based on his research.

During the past thirty years, Bloxham tape-recorded over 400 examples of reincarnation. He has thousands of feet of recordings, much of the material dull and uninteresting, but some of it regarded by experts as providing considerable proof of reincarnation or something very much akin to it. Some background on the man himself may be pertinent: Bloxham served the government in both World Wars, holding the rank of naval lieutenant in the Second World War. Originally he had intended to become a doctor, and started training as a doctor in India, but a bout with typhoid cut short his medical career, and it led him to concentrate on hypno-therapy, something he had been interested in for quite some time.

He was also deeply interested in Eastern and Occult philosophy, and the law of karma. From his childhood, he was convinced of his own earlier incarnation, and was known to have said, "I had always felt that I had lived before." Throughout his life he held fast to his belief in rebirth, his faith being confirmed by his study of reincarnation in the East and the work he was about to do.

Dr. Bloxham's experiments in regression began late in his career, for it was only in 1956 that he decided to use hypnosis to unlock memories of past lives. His first experiment was carried out on a young schoolteacher named Ann Ockenden, who readily entered into hypnotic trance and was eventually regressed back to seven different lives. Bloxham's wife, Dulcie, in order to make his work more well-known, described these first experiments in a book entitled *Who Was Ann Ockenden?*

Another of Bloxham's more notable subjects was Jane Evans, born in 1939, who was able to recall six previous lives, the earliest as a woman who lived in England about AD 286, near Eboracum or Roman York. The most interesting of her regressions was as Rebecca, a Jewish woman of York, who came to a violent end in 1190 during a massacre of the Jews. Jane Evans, incidentally, was a lively and intelligent woman, seemingly of Jewish stock herself, who attended high school, studied history, French and Latin, but not to an advanced level. She had read about Greece and Tibet, and although she never mentioned these two countries in her regressed states, she was interested in ancient times and Eastern religions.

Professor Barrie Dobson, Reader in History at the University of York, whose history of the Jewish massacre of 1190 in York had recently been published—and, yes, many made much of the possibility that Jane had read his book!—was of the opinion that although the language used by Rebecca belonged more to the twentieth century than to medieval England, the account was "true to what we know of the events and times themselves."

Another notable subject of Bloxham's was Graham Huxtable, a

man from Swansea, who regressed two centuries to his life as a gunner's mate on HMS *Aggie,* a frigate under Captain Pearce, then engaged in blockading the coast of Napoleonic France. Under hypnosis, Huxtable dramatically recreated a fight with a French ship off Calais, using archaic slang, and speaking of incidents on board ship which are now obsolete. The mate's leg was shot away by cannon fire—Huxtable re-lived the agony with an intensity that spoke powerfully for the truth of reincarnation. What's more, he gave so many unusual details about naval life at the time, that Earl Mountbatten (who died in 1979) borrowed the tape to play back to experts on naval history. It should be noted that there was, at that time, no record of any ship named HMS *Aggie,* and it was impossible to identify any Captain Pearce who skippered a British frigate in the circumstances described. Years later, however, research instigated by Bloxham uncovered historical records of the HMS *Aggie,* and all the details told by Huxtable held true.

As more serious students begin to probe deeper into the mysteries of hypnotic regression, they—like Bloxham, Stevenson, and literally hundreds of others—find it increasingly difficult to resist the conclusion that there might be more here than meets the eye, that the obvious conclusion of the truth of reincarnation may well explain the curious data that emerges from subjects in trance.

Concluding Thoughts

And so we come full circle. We began by explaining the logic of reincarnation, showing how transmigration can be explained logically and with reference to common sense and analogy. We then went on to elucidate the various world religions—from oldest to newest, i.e., Hinduism, Buddhism, Judaism, Christianity and Islam—showing that the more ancient the religion, the more it held tight to its reincarnationist roots, and that its mystical traditions, in particular, were well aware of its dependence on the doctrine of rebirth to explain its most subtle mysteries. Through interpolation and political maneuvering, various historical figures have tried to undermine the teachings of transmigration, either because it did not fit in with their world view or because they genuinely misunderstood the mystical underpinnings of their own religious tradition. This same scenario exists today, when not only religionists but scientists, too, see reincarnation as an idea that doesn't fit in with their sense of the universe, or they have come to see it as irrelevant and decidedly unscientific.

Nonetheless, we have seen that, as in religion, where orthodox and conservative practitioners who decry the doctrine of rebirth are counterbalanced by deep-thinking mystics who appreciate it, so in science, there are the Ian Stevensons, though few and far between, who show that reincarnation is a teaching with which scientists must reckon. Whether Stevenson—or other scientists who, like him, have come to endorse the doctrine of reincarnation—prove their contentions to the satisfaction of the mainstream or not, he has proven it to his own satisfaction and to the satisfaction of all who take the time to study his work. The reader is requested to look into Stevenson's scientific findings, and to study the religious scriptures and tradition of their choice with an unbiased mind in regard to reincarnation. If the reader does so, I am confident that he or she will thereby put an end to the cycle of birth and death in his or her own life and eventually attain the supreme destination.

ENDNOTES

1 For more on this idea, see ed., H. Byron Earhart, *Religious Traditions of the World* (San Francisco: HarperCollins Publishers, 1990), pp. 280-1.

2 Gary Zukav, *The Dancing Wu Li Masters: An Overview of the New Physics* (New York: Bantam Books, 1980), p. 54.

3 Joe Fisher, op. cit., p. 21.

4 Quoted in Ibid., p. 19.

5 Arthur Berger, "Out of Order Chaos", *Skeptical Inquirer* 14 (1990), p. 392.

6 Jurgen Keil, "New Cases in Burma, Thailand, and Turkey: A Limited Field Study Replication of Some Aspects of Ian Stevenson's Research," *Journal of Scientific Exploration* 5 (1991), pp. 27-55.

If you enjoyed this book we feel sure you will also enjoy our other titles listed at the back. Take a look now!

BIBLIOGRAPHY

Abhedananda Swami. *Doctrine of Karma*. Calcutta: Ramakrishna Vedanta Math, 1944.

Addison, J.T. *Life Beyond Death in the Beliefs of Mankind*. London: Allen & Unwin, 1933.

Albrecht, Mark. "Reincarnation and the Early Church." *Update (A Quarterly Journal of New Religious Movements)* 7 (June 1983): 34-39.

———. *Reincarnation: A Christian Appraisal*. Downers Grove, IL.: InterVarsity, 1982.

Algeo, John. *Reincarnation Explored*. Wheaton, IL.: Theosophical Publishing House, 1987.

Alger, W. R. *A Critical History of the Doctrine of a Future Life*. New York: Greenwood Press, 1968.

Aurobindo, Sri. *The Problem of Rebirth*. Pondicherry, India: Sri Aurobindo Ashram, 1952.

Bayly, C.A. "From Ritual to Ceremony: Death Ritual and Society in Hindu North India Since 1600." In *Mirrors of Mortality: Studies in the Social Histories of Death*, edited by Joachim Whaley. London: Europa Publications, 1981. 154-86

Berg, Philip. *Reincarnation: The Wheels of a Soul*. Jerusalem, Israel, New York: Research Centre of Kabbalah, 1982.

———. *Kabbalah for the Layman*. Volume 1. Jerusalem, Israel, New York: Research Centre of Kabbalah, 1984.

Berger, Arthur and Joyce. *Reincarnation: Fact or Fable?* London: The Aquarian Press, 1991.

Bernstein, Morey. *The Search for Bridey Murphy*. New York: Doubleday, 1965.

Besant, Annie. *Karma*. Madras: Theosophical Publishing House, 1971.

Bhaktisvarupa Damodara Swami. *Fundamental Principles of Reincarnation*. Bombay: Bhaktivedanta Institute, 1979.

Blakiston, Patrick. *The Pre-Existence and Transmigration of Souls*. London: Regency Press, 1970.

Bluck, R.S. "The Phaedrus and Reincarnation." *American Journal of Philology* 89 (April 1958): 156-64.

Bond, George D. "Theravada Buddhism's Meditations on Death and the Symbolism of Initiatory Death," in *History of Religions* 19 (1980): 237-58.

Bowen, Francis. "Christian Metempsychosis." *Princeton Review*, May, 1881

Brandon, S.G.F. *The Judgment of the Dead: An Historical and Comparative Study of the Idea of a Post-Mortem Judgment in the Major Religions*. London: Weidenfeld and Nicolson, 1967.

Brody, Seth. "Reincarnation and the Righteous," *Kabbalah: A Newsletter of Current Research in Jewish Mysticism*, edited by Goodman, Hananya and Krassen, Miles. Volume 3, Number 1 (Fall 1988): 9.

Burke, Abbot George. *May a Christian Believe in Reincarnation?* Oklahoma City, OK: St. George Press, 1984.

Butler, Chris. *Who Are You? Discovering Your Real Identity*. Honolulu: The Identity Institute, 1984.

———. *Reincarnation Explained*. Honolulu: The Identity Institute, 1983.

Chidester, David. *Patterns of Transcendence: Religion, Death, and Dying*. Belmont, CA.: Wadsworth, 1990.

Christie-Murray, David. *Reincarnation: Ancient Beliefs and Modern Evidence*. Great Britain: Prism Press, 1981.

Coming Back: The Science of Reincarnation. Contemporary Vedic Library Series. Los Angeles: Bhaktivedanta Book Trust, 1982.

Cooper, Irving, S. *Reincarnation: The Hope of the World*. Wheaton, IL.: Theosophical Publishing House, 1972.

Cragg, Gerald, R. *The Cambridge Platonists*. New York: Oxford University Press, 1968.

Cranston, Sylvia, and Williams, Carey. *Reincarnation: A New Horizon in Science, Religion, and Society*. New York: Julian Press, 1984.

———. *Reincarnation in World Thought*. New York: The Julian Press, 1967.

Culpepper, Hugo H. Review of *Reincarnation for the Christian*, by Quincy Howe Jr. *Review and Expositor* 72 (Winter 1975):120-21.

Deardorff, James W. *Jesus in India: A Reexamination of Jesus' Asian Traditions in the Light of Evidence Supporting Reincarnation*. San Francisco: International Scholars Publications, 1994.

DeSilva, Lynn A. *Reincarnation in Buddhist and Christian Thought*. Colombo, Sri Lanka: Christian Literature Society of Ceylon, 1968.

Ducasse, C.W. *A Critical Examination of the Belief in Life After Death*. Springfield, IL.: C.C. Thomas, 1960.

Eisler, Robert. *Orpheus the Fisher*. London: Watkins, 1921.

Evans, W.H. *Reincarnation: Fact or Fallacy?* London: Psychic Press, 1957.

Fisher, Joe. *The Case for Reincarnation.* With a Preface by the Dalai Lama. New York: Bantam Books, 1985.

Gallup, George, Jr. *Adventures in Immortality.* New York: McGraw-Hill, 1982.

Geisler, Norman L., and Amano, J. Yutaka. *The Reincarnation Sensation.* Wheaton, Il.: Tyndale House Publishers, 1987.

Grayson, Bobby Kent. *Is Reincarnation Compatible with Christianity? A Historical, Biblical, and Theological Evaluation.* Unpublished Ph.D. dissertation. Southwestern Baptist Theological Seminary, Fort Worth, Texas, September, 1989.

Guirdham, Arthur. *The Cathars and Reincarnation.* London: Neville Spearman, 1970.

Gunaratna, V.F. *Rebirth Explained.* Kandy: Buddhist Publication Society, 1971.

Hall, Manley P. *Reincarnation, The Cycle of Necessity.* Los Angeles: The Philosophical Research Society, 1967.

Hartley, Christine. *A Case for Reincarnation.* London: Robert Hale & Company, 1972.

Head, Joseph, and Cranston, S.L. *Reincarnation: An East-West Anthology.* Wheaton, Il.: The Theosophical Publishing House, 1961.

———. *The Phoenix Fire Mystery.* New York: The Julian Press, 1979.

Hick, John. *Death and Eternal Life.* London: Collins, 1976.

Hodson, Geoffrey. *Reincarnation: Fact or Fallacy?* Wheaton, IL.: Theosophical Publishing House, 1967.

Holck, Frederick H. ed. *Death and Eastern Thought: Understanding Death in Eastern Religions and Philosophies.* Nashville: Abingdon Press, 1974.

Howe, Quincey, Jr. *Reincarnation for the Christian.* Philadelphia: Westminster Press, 1974.

Humphries, Christmas. *Karma and Rebirth.* London: Murray, 1959.

Jung, C.G. Anna Blackwell, trans. *Concerning Rebirth, Collected Works.* 9, 1 New York: Pantheon, 1959.

Kaplan, Steven J., ed. *Concepts of Transmigration.* Lewiston, New York: The Edwin Mellen Press, 1996.

Kapleau, Philip, ed. *The Wheel of Death: A Collection of Writings from Zen Buddhist and Other Sources on Death, Rebirth, Dying.* New York: Harper & Row, 1971.

Kinsley, David. "The Death That Conquers Death: Dying to the World in Medieval Hinduism." In Reynolds and Waugh, eds. *Religious Encounters with*

Death: Insights from the History and Anthropology of Religions. University Park: The Pennsylvania State University Press, 1977. 97-108.

Knipe, David M. "*Sapi—kara—a*: The Hindu Rite of Entry into Heaven." in Reynolds and Waugh, eds., op. cit., 111-24.

Knobloch, Martha. *Reincarnation: The Gospel Truth.* Shippensbburg, PA.: Destiny Image Publishers, 1988.

Kramer, Kenneth. *The Sacred Art of Dying: How World Religions Understand Death.* New York: Paulist Press, 1988.

Kung, Hans. *Eternal Life? Life After Death as a Medical, Philosophical, and Theological Problem.* New York: Doubleday, 1984.

Langley, Noel. *Edgar Cayce on Reincarnation.* New York: Paperback Library, 1967.

Lee, Peter. "Reincarnation in the Christian Tradition." *The Modern Churchman* 23 (Summer 1980):103-17

Leek, Sybil. *Reincarnation, The Second Chance.* New York: Stein & Day, 1974.

Livingston, Marjorie. "Reincarnation, A Historical and Critical Review." *The Aryan Path*, June 1938: 95-299

Long, Herbert Strainge. *A Study of the Doctrine of Metempsychosis in Greece: From Pythagoras to Plato.* Princeton: Princeton University Press, 1948.

Long, J. Bruce. "The Death That Ends Death in Hinduism and Buddhism." In *Death: The Final Stage of Growth.* Ed. Elisabeth Kubler-Ross. Englewood Cliffs, NJ: Prentice-Hall, 1975. 52-72.

MacGregor, Geddes. *Reincarnation in Christianity.* Wheaton, IL.: Theosophical Publishing House, 1978.

———. *Reincarnation as a Christian Hope.* Totowa, New Jersey: Barnes & Noble Imports, 1982.

———. *The Christening of Karma: The Secret of Evolution.* Wheaton, IL.: Theosophical Publishing House, 1984.

Mead, G.R.S. "The Reincarnationists of Early Christendom." *The Quest* (April 1914): 88-101.

Moody, Raymond A. *Life After Life.* New York: Bantam, 1975.

Moore, C.H. *Ancient Beliefs in the Immortality of the Soul.* New York: Cooper Square Publishers, Inc., 1963.

Moore, G.F. *Metempsychosis.* Cambridge: Harvard University Press, 1914.

Morey, Robert A. *Reincarnation and Christianity.* Minneapolis, MN: Bethany House Publishers, 1980.

Muller, Karl E. *Reincarnation Based on Facts*. London, Psychic Press, 1970.

Nemoy, Leon. "Biblical Quasi-Evidence for the Transmigration of Souls." *Journal of Biblical Literature* 59 (June 1940):159-68.

Neufeldt, Ronald W. *Karma and Rebirth: Post Classical Developments*. Albany: State University of New York Press, 1986.

Nevins, Albert J. *Life After Death: A Catholic Understanding*. Huntington, IN: Our Sunday Visitor, Inc., 1983.

O'Flaherty, Wendy D., ed. *Karma and Rebirth in Classical Indian Traditions*. Berkeley: University of California Press, 1980.

———. *The Origins of Evil in Hindu Mythology*. Berkeley: University of California Press, 1976.

Parrinder, E.G. "Varieties of Belief in Reincarnation." *The Hibbert Journal*, April 1957.

Prabhupada, A.C. Bhaktivedanta Swami. *Bhagavad-gita As It Is*. New York: Collier Books, 1972.

———. *The Laws of Nature: An Infallible Justice*. Los Angeles: Bhaktivedanta Book Trust, 1991.

———. *A Second Chance: The Story of a Near-Death Experience*. Los Angeles: Bhaktivedanta Book Trust, 1991.

Prophet, Elizabeth Clare. *Reincarnation: The Missing Link in Christianity*. Corwin Springs, MT: Summit UP, 1997.

Pryse, James M. *Reincarnation in the New Testament*. New York: Elliott B. Page & Co., 1900, reprint, 1965.

Reichenbach, Bruce R. *The Law of Karma*. Honolulu: University of Hawaii Press, 1991.

Reyes, Benito F. *Scientific Evidence of the Existence of the Soul*. Wheaton, IL.: Theosophical Publishing House, 1970.

Reyna, Ruth. *Reincarnation and Science*. New Delhi: Sterling Publishers, 1975.

Rhine, Louisa E. "Review of Ian Stevenson, *Twenty Cases Suggestive of Reincarnation*." *The Journal of Parapsychology* (December 1966):265.

Robillard, Edmond. *Reincarnation: Illusion or Reality?* New York: Alba House, 1982.

Rouse, W.H.D., ed. *The Jatakas, or Stories of the Buddha's Former Births*. Cambridge: Oxford University Press, 1910.

Schaya, Leo. *The Universal Meaning of the Kabbalah*. London: Unwin Hyman, Ltd., 1989.

Scholem, Gershom. *On the Mystical Shape of the Godhead: Basic Concepts in the Kabbalah*. New York: Schocken Books, 1991, reprint.

Sewell, H.B. *An Assessment of Ideological Conflict Between Reincarnation and Karma Notions and Fundamental Notions in Christian Doctrine*. Unpublished Ph.D. dissertation, University of Lancaster, May 1978.

Sharma, I.C. *Cayce, Karma and Reincarnation*. New York: Harper & Row, 1975.

Shirley, Ralph. *The Problem of Rebirth*. London: Rider & Company, 1938.

Snyder, John. *Reincarnation vs. Resurrection*. Chicago: Moody Press, 1984.

Sonsino, Rifat, and Daniel B. Syme. *What Happens After I Die? Jewish Views of Life After Death*. New York: UAHC Press, 1990.

Steiner, Rudolph. *Reincarnation and Immortality*. New York: Multi-media Publishing Corporation, 1974.

Stevenson, Ian. "The Evidence for Survival from Claimed Memories of Former Incarnations." *Journal of the American Society for Psychical Research* 54 (1960):. 51-71, 95-117.

———. "Reincarnation: Field Studies and Theoretical Issues." *Handbook of Parapsychology*. Ed. Benjamin B. Wolman. New York: Van Nostrand Reinhold Company, 1977. 631-63.

———. *Cases of the Reincarnation Type, Vol. 1, Ten Cases in India*. Charlottesville: University Press of Virginia, 1975.

———. *Twenty Cases Suggestive of Reincarnation*. Charlottesville: University Press of Virginia, 1966.

Story, Francis. *Rebirth as Doctrine and Experience*. Sri Lanka: Buddhist Publication Society, 1975.

Switala, William J. *Reincarnation Reexamined*. New York: Carlton Press, Inc., 1972.

Tatz, Mark, and Jody Kent. *Rebirth: The Tibetan Game of Liberation*. New York: Anchor Press, 1977.

Toynbee, Arnold, ed. *Life After Death*. London: Weidenfeld & Nicolson, 1976.

Tull, Herman W. *The Vedic Origins of Karma*. Albany: State University of New York Press, 1989.

Underwood, Peter, and Leonard Wilder. *Lives to Remember*. London: Robert Hale, 1975.

Walker, Benjamin. *Masks of the Soul: The Facts Behind Reincarnation*. Wellingborough, Northamptonshire: The Aquarian Press, 1981.

Walker, E.D. *Reincarnation, A Study of Forgotten Truth*. London: William Ryder & Son, 1913.

Weatherhead, Leslie. *The Case for Reincarnation*. Burgh Heath, Tadworth: M.C. Peto, 1960.

Willson, Martin. *Rebirth and the Western Buddhist*. London: Wisdom Publications, 1987.

Yevtic, Paul. *Karma and Reincarnation in Hindu Religion and Philosophy*. London: Luzac and Company, 1927.

Index

Abdi, M. H., 93
Abhidhamma, 48
Abraham, 57
Abulafia, Abraham, 58
Adam, 57
Albigenses, 72
Allah, 89, 91
American Society for Physical
    Research, 98
Apollonius, 14
Aquinas, Thomas, 19
Arabia, 92
Aristotle, 18, 82, 95
Aristotelian-Thomistic view, 19
Arnobius, 78
Ashlag, Yahuda, 58
Association for Research and
    Enlightenment, 70
Atharva Veda, 23
Augustine, Saint, 78, 83

Babism, 94
Bar Hiyya, Abraham, 61
Beausobre, Isaac de, 79
Beck, Guy L., 35-36
Belief in a Future Life, 8-9
Ben Daud, Abraham, 62
Ben David, Anan, 60
Ben Hananiah, Joshua, 63
Ben Israel, Menasah, 61
Ben Pandira, Jehoshuah, 56
Ben Yosef al-Fayyumi, Saadia, 62
Berger, Arthur, 102-104
Bhagavad-gita, 17, 23, 30-35
Bhagavata-purana, 23, 27-30
Bhava Chakra, 46-48
Bible, 53-55. See also under:
    Christianity and reincarnation;
    names of biblical books
Bloxham, Amall, 104-106
Bloxham, Dulcie, 105
Bogomils, 72

About the author

Steven J. Rosen is the author of twelve books on metaphysical subjects, including the popular interreligious books, *OM Shalom* and *East-West Dialogues*. Having published with three of India's prominent publishers — KLM Firma (*Archeology and the Vaishnava Tradition: The Pre-Christian Roots of Krishna Worship*, Calcutta: 1989); Munshiram Manoharlal (*Passage From India: The Life and Times of His Divine Grace A. C. Bhaktivedanta Swami Prabhupada*, Delhi: 1992); and Motilal Banarsidass (*Vaishnavism: Contemporary Scholars Discuss the Gaudiya Tradition*, Delhi: 1994, reprint) — he has developed an important voice in the Indian religious community. He is editor-in-chief of the *Journal of Vaishnava Studies*, an academic quarterly that is esteemed and supported by scholars worldwide.

Diet For Transcendence

Vegetarianism and the World Religions

by Steven Rosen

$11.95 ISBN #1-887089-05-5
6"x 9", paper 156 pgs.

"Steven Rosen takes us on a fascinating journey back in time to explore the essential and often misunderstood roots of the world's major religious traditions, to discover how vegetarianism was a cherished part of their philosophy and practice."

Nathaniel Altman,
Author, *Eating for Life*

Following the Path of Kindness

This is reinforcement and inspiration for the 86% of the American population that is making a conscious effort to improve their diets by consuming more fruits and vegetables. Following an introductory overview of the physiological, environmental and economic reasons for adopting a vegetarian diet, Steven Rosen considers vegetarianism in Christianity, Judaism, Islam, Hinduism and Buddhism. The results of his research will come as a surprise to many religious adherents. You'll discover how vegetarianism is an ideal shared by all religions which teach mercy and respect for all creatures.

Diet for Transcendence is the perfect gift for your loved ones or yourself. Order your copies today!

Available from your local bookseller, or just fill out the order form in back and fax it, or call us toll free at:
1-888-TORCHLT (867-2458) Fax: (209) 337-2354

Book Order Form _____

☎ Telephone orders: Call 1-888-TORCHLT (1-888-867-2458).
Have your VISA or MasterCard ready.

✳ FAX orders: 209-337-2354

✉ Postal orders: Torchlight Publishing   PO Box 52
Badger CA 93603-0052 USA

▲ World Wide Web: www.torchlightpub.com

Please send the following: QTY

• **The Reincarnation Controversy,** by Steven Rosen $11.95 x ___ = $ _____

• **Diet for Transcendence**, by Steven Rosen $11.95 x ___ = $ _____

Sales Tax: (CA residents add 7.75%) . . . . .$ _____

S/H (see below) . . . .$ _____

TOTAL . . . . $ _____

◯ Please send me more information on other books published by Torchlight Publishing.

Company: _____

Name: _____

Address: _____

City:_____ State_____ Zip_____

(I understand that I may return any books for a full refund — for any reason,
no questions asked.)

Payment:

◯ Check/money order enclosed   ◯ VISA   ◯ MasterCard

Card Number: _____

Name on Card: _____ Exp. date_____

Signature: _____

Shipping and handling:

USA : $3.00 for first book and $1.75 for each additional book. Air mail per book (USA only) — $4.00
Canada : $5.00 for first book and $2.50 for each additional book
Foreign countries: $8.00 for first book, $4.00 for each additional book.
Surface shipping may take 3-4 weeks. Foreign orders please allow 6-8 weeks for delivery.